The Magician
and the Cinema

The Magician
and the Cinema

Erik Barnouw

New York · Oxford
OXFORD UNIVERSITY PRESS
1981

Library of Congress Cataloging in Publication Data

Barnouw, Erik, 1908-
The magician and the cinema.

Bibliography: p.
Includes index.
1. Cinematography, Trick—History. 2. Conjuring—History. I. Title.
TR858.B37   778.5'345   80-27342
ISBN 0-19-502918-6
9 8 7 6 5 4 3 2 1

Printed in the United States of America

If this be magic, let it be an art
Lawful as eating.
> —Shakespeare

Preface

Ladies and gentlemen . . .

While in high school, many years ago, I was hired by the magician John Mulholland to catalog his books on magic. I was fourteen. Each Saturday I went to his place to make out cards; and, while leafing through the books, made the acquaintance of fascinating characters—people like Robert-Houdin, the "Father of Modern Magic"; John Henry Anderson, "Wizard of the North"; Maskelyne and Devant of "England's Home of Mystery"; Herrmann the Great; Félicien Trewey; Georges Méliès, who took over Robert-Houdin's magic theatre; and of course the incredible Houdini. I was paid by the card, so the browsing I did was at my expense, not Mulholland's. I even had a chance to browse through the mysterious "locked books" of Will Goldston, available only to magicians. The key was there—I had to use it to do the cataloging.

The collection was international, and perhaps that is a reason I got the job. My family had recently arrived from Holland; I could speak Dutch and had some knowledge of French and German—languages well represented in the collection. The family had met Mulholland soon after arrival.

Mulholland, a towering, low-key, urbane performer, loved to talk about his books and where he had found them. Sometimes he talked about magicians he knew, and their favorite pastime of exposing spiritualists. He had many books about spiritualists—my favorite title was *Eusapia Palladino and Her Phenomena*. Once Mulholland involved me in a supper party with three other magicians. Around midnight, over Welsh rarebit, they began to dazzle each other with legerdemain. I got home at 4 a.m. My mother was terrified.

Mulholland's magic collection was one of the largest, considered second only to that of Houdini, whom Mulholland knew well. I saw Mulholland occasionally during the following decades. He became editor of *The Sphinx*, official organ of the Society of American Magicians. His collection kept growing. At our last meeting—by chance, on Broadway—he mentioned his decision to give his collection to the Players Club. By that time I was deeply involved in the history of mass media and supervising film studies at Columbia University. I mentioned to Mulholland how often, in exploring film history, I had come across names I had first met in his books. Had magicians perhaps had a larger role in the evolution of moving pictures than was generally recognized? He said: "That's a wonderful subject. Come to my place and I'll drag out a couple of dozen books that have a bearing on it."

He died before I could make that trip. But eventually I did visit the Players Club to track down the books he must have had in mind; and later, when I left the Columbia University campus for the Library of Congress, I had a chance to pursue the search in the Houdini Collection, a large part of which had come to rest there.

That is the genesis of *The Magician and the Cinema*. Much of it derives from the literature of magic, a source most film historians have neglected. I am grateful to Louis A. Rachow of the Players Club, curator of the Mulholland Collection, and to Leonard Beck of the Library of Congress, curator of its Houdini Collection, for their help. I must also acknowledge a debt to film historians who have explored the film-magic connection, and whose works have provided valuable leads. These would include especially Jacques Deslandes and Jacques Richard, authors of *Histoire comparée du cinéma;* John Barnes of the Barnes Museum of Cinematography of St. Ives, England, publishers of the enlightening catalogs *Optical Projection* and *Precursors of the Cinema;* two able biographers of Méliès, Paul Hammond of *Marvellous Méliès* and John Frazer of *Artificially Arranged Scenes;* and Kemp Niver, whose work with the Paper Print Collection of the Library of Congress has salvaged many of the early films—the incunabula of film history—that help to tell this story. I must also thank, again and again, my colleagues at the Motion Picture, Broadcasting and Recorded Sound Division of the Library of Congress.

Washington, D.C.   Erik Barnouw
February 1981

Contents

The Magician
and the Cinema

1

The Magician

Entertainment of Wonders and
Conflux of Apparent Miracles
—19th-Century magic poster

The magician was King of Entertainment. In special Magic Theatres or on Grand Tours, he astounded. His shows were high spots of family trips. He turned a man into a skeleton, then back into a man. A woman disappeared in a puff of smoke, or she was burned alive on the stage, to arise presently from her ashes. The shows included robots who could play the violin or read people's minds. There were fantastic "illusions" like rocket trips to the moon, descents into hell, and visits to mermaids under the sea. The magician let you know it was all skill, aided by science, nothing supernatural, no sorcery—but you could believe what you liked.

As a final sensational climax, there might be a decapitation. The magician cut off somebody's head and placed it on a tray or table. Then he would go to attend to the headless body. Meanwhile the severed head would suddenly open its eyes and start to talk. This was called, long before television, the "talking head." It couldn't fail.

Some magicians did "self-capitation." One wizard even took his final bow headless, with his own severed head in one hand, his wife's in the other.

To all these wonders, in the year 1896, magicians on every continent suddenly added a new and astounding attraction—the miracle of the century, the wonder of the world—"living pictures." Within months it dominated all other wonders.

Harry Kellar poster, 1897   (*Library of Congress*)

Magician's grand finale, *ca.* 1890—A headless Carl Hertz holds severed heads of self and wife (*Library of Congress*)

The role of the magician in early cinema has been neglected by film scholars, with some notable exceptions. Many people find it difficult to think of film in the context of magic. But the first viewers had no trouble on that score. As trains rushed by them, and living images of King, Kaiser, and Maharaja walked before them, they knew they were seeing things that could not be. We today, having come to accept such things as "reality," have lost the magic of them. They knew they were seeing magic.

The magician was indeed a film pioneer. A virtuoso technician, he had already contributed importantly to the prehistory of cinema. For more than a century he had offered illusions based on projected images, which often made unsuspected use of concealed "magic lanterns." With these he could already do astounding things, and the Cinématographe was merely the next logical step. The magician at once grasped its ramifications, and he carried it within months throughout the world. The rapid diffusion of the motion picture owes much to the magician's whirlwind travels. Many magicians, of many countries, became involved.

Genesis of "special effects"—above and on facing page, contributions of Georges Méliès

A Trip to the Moon, 1902   (Museum of Modern Art, New York)

Some plunged into film making, transferring to the screen some of their grandest moments—sensing, perhaps, a chance at immortality on celluloid. They played a pioneer role in animation, and they set in motion the "trick" film, which laid the foundations for the field of "special effects" in the modern cinema. The *Star Wars* saga derives its genes from the 1902 *A Trip to the Moon*.

Yet these early film activities of magicians are now little known, and the reason may not be mysterious. Much of the story has lain buried in the annals of magic—and for good reason. For magicians the plunge into cinema proved an eventual disaster. The touring magician who took films to South Africa or Australia or China as part of his magic repertoire found, just a few years

The Impossible Voyage, 1904   (*Library of Congress*)

The Conquest of the Pole, 1912   (*Museum of Modern Art, New York*)

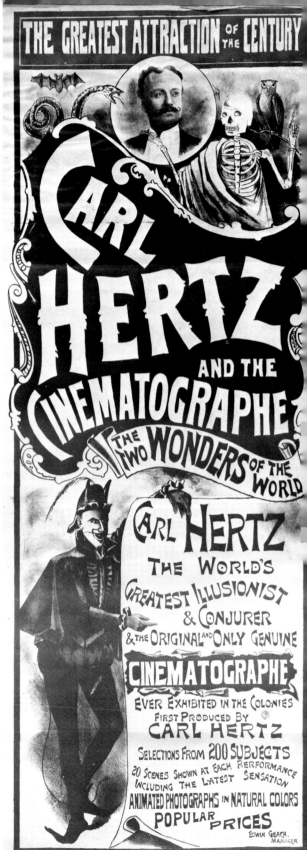

Carl Hertz brings new magic to Melbourne—Australia's first film poster, 1896 *(Library of Congress)*

later, that the theatres no longer wanted the repertoire, just the film portion. Cinema had become a powerful robot ousting its former master. And the transfer to the screen of the magician's most sensational illusions—disappearances, bizarre transformations and beheadings—proved ultimately catastrophic for magicians. Anyone with a camera and a splicer could produce the same miracles, and did. The sensations ceased to be sensational. Even on stage they began to seem stale. The magician found he had been helping to destroy his own profession. Many magicians survived as magicians, in some cases by stressing the ancient skills of prestidigitation, rather than equipment trickery. Others merged into the world of film and took part in a new evolution of the extraordinary.

This book seeks to recapture the brief period when the history of magic and the history of cinema intersected, to the swift and worldwide benefit of cinema, and the discomfiture of the world of magic.

The
Science Wizards

. . . magic casements, opening on the foam
Of perilous seas. . . .

—Keats

Nineteenth-century magicians brought to their profession a zest-
ful appetite for science. Most were grounded in ancient varieties
of legerdemain, and combined them with such specialties as
juggling, escapology, shadowgraphy, chalk-talk, ventriloquism,
mind-reading or instant-transformation acts. But they also found,
in that century of prolific invention, that every new scientific invention had magic possibilities. The magician made it his business to stay a step or two ahead of public understanding of science. New tricks came as fast as inventions. By their very nature,
many of these tricks had a short life, as public understanding
caught up with them.

In the 1840s the Austrian magician Ludwig Döbler began his
act by walking out onto a dark stage. Apologizing to the audience
for the lack of illumination, he then fired a pistol, which seemed
to light the innumerable candles on his stage simultaneously.
This sensational opening, also used by the French magician
Philippe, was obviously good for only a short time.

Mysteries of electricity were likewise exploited by the French
magician Jean Eugène Robert-Houdin, "the father of modern
magic"—whose fame was to inspire the Hungarian-born Ehrich
Weiss to adopt the name Houdini. A celebrated moment in Robert-Houdin's life came during an 1856 visit to Algeria, made at
the request of the French government. The colony was restless,
stirred to a rebellious state by wonder-performing holy men, the

marabouts. The government hoped that Robert-Houdin could persuade the Algerians that the French had far more powerful magic, and that resistance or insurrection would prove futile.

Performing in Algiers, Robert-Houdin had a trunk brought onto the stage and invited marabouts in the audience to lift it, which they did with ease. Robert-Houdin then said that he would, by magic, take away their powers. After suitable abracadabra he invited the marabouts to lift the trunk again, which they could not do, despite fantastic exertions. Having watched their failure, Robert-Houdin had the trunk carried off by his assistants. It had a metal bottom. Under the stage he had placed a powerful electromagnet, activated for the climax of the performance.[1]

Robert-Houdin had been trained as a watchmaker and had invented an electric clock. His house was full of electric gadgets to delight the visitor. An alarm clock would wake the guest, and at the same moment light a candle for him. The skills developed in such pursuits were key elements in Robert-Houdin's career. Even before turning to magic he had created robots controlled by clockwork, able to perform such feats as playing chess, solving mathematical problems, or drawing silhouettes. Later the robots—they were called "automata" at the time—became a feature of his magic performances. In 1845 he founded in Paris the Théâtre Robert-Houdin, which showed magic for over seventy years, continuing long after the death of its founder. The theatre workshops produced a continual series of new illusions, including optical effects using multiple magic lanterns. The optical creations became especially important after 1888, when the Théâtre Robert-Houdin came under the ownership and management of Georges Méliès. Under him the workshops made film as well as theatre history.

In London the Egyptian Hall, "England's Home of Mystery," had a similar evolution. Its shows began in 1873 and continued for over half a century, with one change of location. The co-founder John Nevil Maskelyne had, like Robert-Houdin, a watchmaking background and became a prolific inventor of magic mechanisms, occasionally digressing into other inventions. He was at the same time a skilled prestidigitator and plate-spinner. His co-founder, George Alfred Cooke, had been a cabinetmaker and served the partnership with many trick cabinets for "disappearances" and other illusions. The inventing of new apparatus for "England's Home of Mystery" was carried on in workshops

Coffre Lourd (The Heavy Trunk)—engraving celebrating Robert-Houdin's Algerian coup   (*Courtesy Milbourne Christopher*)

13

Boulevard des Italiens, Paris, 1895—at right, the Théâtre Robert-Houdin (*National Film Archive, London*)

that by the end of the century were described by the magician Jasper Maskelyne, grandson of John Nevil Maskelyne, as "so extensive as to dwarf that part of the Egyptian Hall devoted to public performances."[2] As at the Théâtre Robert-Houdin, robots played a part in the shows. The first robot, called Psycho, could play whist; a lady robot called Zoe drew profiles of spectators. Celebrated magicians made guest appearances. One of them, the stylish David Devant, became a regular performer in 1893 and a partner a few years later. His range of skills included shadowgraphy, a specialty that helped to propel him—and the Egyptian Hall—into early film history.

John Nevil Maskelyne   (*National Film Archive, London*)

Egyptian Hall, 1896 (*Library of Congress*)

The participation of these and other magic theatres in the debut of cinema can be seen as the logical outcome of more than a century of scientific magic, in which optics were always important. A central role in the optical magic was played by the extraordinary magic lantern. Its role was not a recognized one; magic performers were necessarily secretive about their methods, and the general public was scarcely aware of the magic lantern as such until its use by lecturers in the late decades of the nineteenth century, when it came to be used visibly. Long before that, magicians were using it covertly for spectacular effect.

The magic lantern had begun its entertainment career in a modest way in the seventeenth century.[3] Its principles had been discussed by the Jesuit scholar Athanasius Kircher in the 1646 edition of his book *Ars Magna Lucis et Umbrae* (The Great Art of Light and Shadow) and it was described in detail in 1659 by the Dutch scientist Christian Huygens. In the 1660s and 1670s the Danish Thomas Rasmussen Walgersten, who had studied in the Netherlands, gave magic-lantern demonstrations to small groups in various parts of Europe. The English optician and telescope maker Richard Reeves took an interest in the device, and in this connection he is mentioned in a Samuel Pepys diary entry of August 19, 1666:

> . . . by and by comes by agreement Mr. Reeves. . . . He did also bring a lantern with pictures in glass, to make strange things to appear on a wall, very pretty.

Pepys purchased "the lantern that shows tricks." But such entertainment uses were private, and for the well-to-do. It was in the 1790s that the magic lantern suddenly acquired a virtuoso role in public entertainment. The genius behind this development was a Belgian experimenter named Étienne Gaspard Robert, who as a showman took the name Robertson.

The Fantasms

Enter these enchanted woods,
You who dare.

—Meredith

In his native Liège, Robertson began to startle audiences with a bone-chilling performance called *Fantasmagorie*, which he took to Paris about 1794. In 1797, when he acquired as his setting an abandoned chapel on the grounds of an old Capuchin monastery, surrounded by ancient tombs, he scored an historic success. Audiences entered through cavernous corridors, marked with strange symbols, and came on a dimly lit chamber decorated with skulls; effects of thunder, sepulchral music, and tolling bells helped set the mood. Coal burned in braziers. Robertson gave a preliminary discourse, denouncing charlatans and their bogus apparitions and promising something superior. He tossed some chemicals on the braziers, causing columns of smoke to rise. The single lamp flickered out, putting the audience in almost total darkness. Then, onto the smoke arising from the braziers, images were projected from concealed magic lanterns. They included human forms and unearthly spectral shapes. The images came from glass slides, but the movements of the smoke gave them a ghoulish kind of life. Among these apparitions were men and women who had died in the French Revolution, such as Danton, Marat, Robespierre. Their faces, with inscrutably changing expressions, would suddenly appear in the spirals of smoke. Some spectators sank to their knees, convinced they were in the presence of the supernatural. Robertson climaxed his performance with the projected image of a skeleton, "the fate that awaits us all." So powerful was the impact of his apparitions that authorities for a time interfered. Robertson had to be careful about his selection of ghosts.[4]

Robertson's *Fantasmagorie*—engraving depicting projections onto smoke that astounded Paris audiences in the 1790s. The engraving appears as frontispiece in Robertson's *Mémoires*, published 1831. (*Library of Congress*)

"The Fate That Awaits Us All"—Robertson's climactic projection (*Columbia University*)

Robertson used rear projection, which made it easy to keep audiences unaware of the lanterns. In addition to projection onto smoke, he developed a technique for projecting onto layers of gauze, which he soaked in wax and ironed to achieve the right translucency for rear projection. The gauze was hidden from the audience at the start of the show by a black curtain, which was opened in darkness just before the projections. The audience was apparently unaware of the existence of the translucent screen. An important aspect of Robertson's technique was his treatment of the slides. The area around the image was totally blacked out, so that a projected figure had no environment of its own. It seemed to hang in air. Spectators could not tell its distance from them, and sometimes reached out to it. Another aspect was that the lantern was mounted on a sliding arrangement. By moving it forward, while adjusting the focus, Robertson could make the image grow, and give spectators the feeling it was about to overwhelm them, until it suddenly blurred out of existence. By pulling back, he could make it shrink into disappearance. Each effect had its own dramatic possibilities.

Robertson's *Fantasmagorie* ran in Paris for six years. It was so successful that his secrets were inevitably purloined and his effects imitated. Similar performances erupted far and wide—a preview of the later spectacular diffusion of cinema. Indeed, *Fantasmagorie* had a cinematic quality.

In 1801 the magician Paul de Philipstahl brought his version to London, spelling it *Phantasmagoria*. It ran there two years and

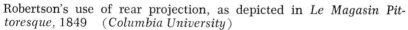

Robertson's use of rear projection, as depicted in *Le Magasin Pittoresque*, 1849 (*Columbia University*)

later had an Edinburgh run. Hewing closely to the Robertson formula, Philipstahl denounced "artful impostors" and said his show was designed "to open the Eyes of those who still foster an absurd belief in Ghosts and Disembodied Spirits." He, like Robertson, aligned himself with science. But then he proceeded to call up apparitions of the "Dead or Absent."

New Yorkers saw a *Phantasmagoria* in 1803; a rash of similar shows under various entrepreneurs followed in other cities, usually with the same title. Charles Pecor, in his survey of American magic based on the contemporary press, mentions *Phantasmagoria* shows in Baltimore, Boston, Cincinnati, Covington, Philadelphia, Providence, Salem (Mass.), and Savannah. An 1807 performance in Boston by a "Mr. Martin," who proclaimed his act as "The Truly Original Phantasmagoria," caused the Columbian Museum to burn down.[5] But this did not halt the *Phantasmagoria* epidemic. Robertson himself, after spending intervening years on balloon experimentation, resumed his show career and made American appearances in 1825 and 1834.[6]

Spirit raisers were not always welcome. The Philadelphia-born magician Jacob Meyer, who had toured his magic throughout Europe as Philadelphus Philadelphia, and who had added spirit raising to his repertoire, found his act halted in Vienna—perhaps as a fire-prevention measure, but perhaps for political reasons. He may have raised questionable spirits. The German-born Andrew Oehler ran into worse trouble in Mexico: the ghosts he raised there in 1806 landed him in a dungeon, fed with morsels lowered from above. Eventually released, he forswore magic and settled in the United States. He described his ordeal in *The Life, Adventures, and Unparalleled Sufferings of Andrew Oehler,* published in Trenton, N.J., in 1811. It reveals in explicit detail his ghost technology—clearly derived from Robertson.[7]

In the United States, *Phantasmagoria* acquired indigenous aspects. In 1808 the New York *Post,* reviewing a New York performance, mentions that its "fantoms" included Washington, Jefferson, Adams, Hancock, and Robert Morris.[8] Advancement to "fantomhood" was premature in several of these cases. Such problems could be solved by use of Philipstahl's promotional phrase "apparitions of the Dead or Absent."

Projections onto smoke could be used for effects other than apparitions. The 1808 New York *Phantasmagoria* program included "Eruption of Mt. Vesuvius," and others reenacted spectacular fires reported in the news. These edged the technique

PHANTASMAGORIA,

THIS and every EVENING till further Notice,

AT THE

LYCEUM, STRAND.

As the Advertisement of various Exhibitions under the above Title, may possibly mislead the unsuspecting Part o. the Public (and particularly Strangers from the Country) in their Opinion of the ORIGINAL PHANTASMAGORIA, M. DE PHILIPSTHAL, the Inventor, begs Leave to state that they have no Connexion whatever with his Performances. The *utmost Efforts* of Imitators have not been able to produce the Effect intended; and he is too grateful for the liberal Encouragement he has received in the Metropolis, not to caution the Public against those *spurious Copies*, which, falling of the Perfection they assume, can only disgust and disappoint the Spectators.

M. DE PHILIPSTHAL

Will have the Honour to EXHIBIT (as usual) his

Optical Illusions and Mechanical Pieces of Art.

At the LYCEUM, and at no other Place of Exhibition in London.

SELECT PARTIES may be accommodated with a MORNING REPRESENTATION at any appointed Hour, on sending timely Notice.

To prevent Mistakes, the Public are requested to notice, that the PHANTASMAGORIA is on the Left-hand, on the Ground Floor, and the ÆGYPTIANA on the Right-hand, up Stairs.

The OPTICAL PART of the EXHIBITION

Will introduce the PHANTOMS or APPARITIONS of the DEAD or ABSENT, in a way more completely illusive than has ever been offered to the Eye in a public Theatre, as the Objects freely originate in the Air, and unfold themselves under various Forms and Sizes, such as Imagination alone has hitherto painted them, occasionally assuming the Figure and most perfect Resemblance of the Heroes and other distinguished Characters of past and present Times.

This SPECTROLOGY, which professes to expose the Practices of artful Impostors and pretended Exorcists, and to open the Eyes of those who still foster an absurd Belief in GHOSTS or DISEMBODIED SPIRITS, will, it is presumed, afford also to the Spectator an interesting and pleasing Entertainment; and in order to render these Apparitions more interesting, they will be introduced during the Progress of a tremendous Thunder Storm, accompanied with vivid Lightning, Hail, Wind, &c.

The MECHANICAL PIECES of ART

Include the following *principal Objects, a more detailed* Account of which will be given during their Exhibition: viz.

Two elegant ROPE DANCERS, the one, representing a Spaniard nearly Six Feet high, will display several Astonishing Feats on the Rope, mark the Time of the Music with a small Whistle, smoke his Pipe, &c.—The other, called *Pajazzo*, being the Figure of a young sprightly Boy, will surpass the former in Skill and Agility.

The INGENIOUS SELF-DEFENDING CHEST—The superior Excellence and Utility of this Piece of Mechanism is, that the Proprietor has always a Safe-guard against Depredators; for the concealed Battery of *Four Pieces of Artillery* only appears and discharges itself when a Stranger tries to force open the Chest.—This has been acknowledged by several Professional Men to be a *Master-piece of Mechanism,* and may with equal Advantage be applied to the Protection of Property in Counting-houses, Post Chaises, &c.

The MECHANICAL PEACOCK, which so exactly imitates the Actions of that stately Bird, that it has frequently been thought Alive. It eats, drinks, &c. at command, unfold its Tail in a brilliant Circle, and in every respect seems endowed with an intuitive Power of attending to the Thoughts of the Company.

The BEAUTIFUL COSSACK, enclosed in a small Box, opens it when ordered, and presents herself to the Spectators in a black Habit; which, as soon as desired, she changes with astonishing Quickness into a most Elegant Gala Dress, compliments the Company, and dances after the Manner of the Cossacks, she will also resolve different Questions. &c. &c.

The SELF-IMPELLED WINDMILL, which is put in Motion, or stands still by the most momentary Signal from the Spectators, and in a Manner which apparently does away the Idea of all Mechanical Agency.

The whole to conclude with a superb OPTICAL and MECHANICAL FIRE-WORK, replete with a Variety of brilliant and fanciful Changes.

₊ *Doors to be opened at SEVEN o'Clock, the Commencement at EIGHT.*

BOXES, 4s.—PIT, 2s.

The magician Philipstahl brings a *Phantasmagoria* to London—an 1803 poster   (*Library of Congress*)

The persistence of *Phantasmagoria*—items from Houdini scrapbooks

Houdini collected, via gift or purchase, the memorabilia of innumerable magicians. *Above,* the magician Gyngell conjures up a skeleton *à la* Robertson. Facing page, smoke magic by the later Laurant, as depicted in his posters. (*Library of Congress*)

toward a journalistic stance, but in general the machinery encouraged a trend to the spectral or macabre. The many magic acts in which people—usually women—were burned alive in sight of the audience probably involved variations of the *Phantasmagoria* technique. The illusion required a carefully devised moment in which the supposed victim was replaced by a projection onto billowing smoke. The smoke itself could help mask the maneuver.*

Magicians were not alone in seizing the *Phantasmagoria* procedure. Mediums apparently found a market for calling up the dead, to make fleeting appearances for the comfort of the living. The apparitions, similar to those offered by magicians, differed mainly in claims made for them. The mediums were constantly denounced by the magicians. Such disputes continued throughout the century, as fantasms in various forms continued to grip popular attention.

* Variations have never quite died out. In *Magic Shadows,* p. 79, Martin Quigley, Jr., quotes a World War II Associated Press bulletin to the effect that "Tommies manning an outpost during the night suddenly saw an image of the Virgin Mary appear in the clouds, with her arms outstretched in entreaty. The commander sent out a patrol, which returned with the information that the Germans were projecting the image from a machine on the ground" (Feb. 15, 1940).

The disputes brought into new focus the old philosophical issue between "natural" magic—supposedly used for instructive amusement and scientific enlightenment—and exploitative magic using or claiming supernatural means, akin to sorcery and witchcraft. The line between was never clear and remained problematical. But the issue was discussed by David Brewster in his celebrated *Letters on Natural Magic*. Brewster, who gave a detailed

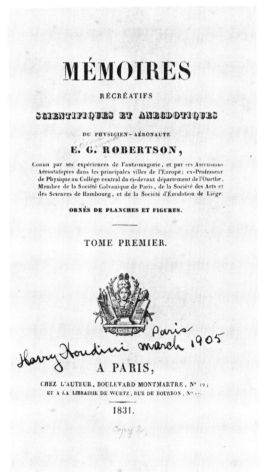

Title page of Robertson's *Mémoires*, 1831—Houdini's copy (*Library of Congress*)

description of a Philipstahl performance, was convinced that projection of images onto smoke was used by priests in ancient times to awe and control worshipers, and that their technique involved a concave mirror to focus light—creating, in effect, a primitive magic lantern. Thus Robertson's illusion, so up-to-date in technology, was seen to have its own prehistory.[9]

In 1831 Étienne Gaspard Robertson published his *Mémoires*, in which he discussed in detail his secrets and his inability to protect them from piracy. By that time a new technical breakthrough was shifting attention to effects of a similar kind but far more precise, and moving further in the direction of cinema.

Until that time, projection effects had been fueled mainly by oil. The invention of limelight about 1820 introduced far more powerful light, that could be directed and focused. By 1840 it was used in theatres. For the magician it opened a whole new range of optical effects and illusions, including new apparitions. Their development was associated with the magician Robin, who had been born in the Netherlands but established his own magic theatre in Paris, the Théâtre Robin—chief rival, for a time, of the Théâtre Robert-Houdin—and with London's Royal Polytechnic Institution, which opened in 1838 and became the locale for spectacular lantern shows and sideshows.

A Polytechnic performance sometimes utilized an enormous sheet of glass tilted at a 45° angle to the stage. Through the control of light this could at one moment allow a view of whatever was behind it, and the next moment show (instead or in addition) a different image, generally projected from below, as from an orchestra pit. The audience was not conscious of the glass sheet as such. The stage could now seem to be occupied by people actually on the stage, and by others not there at all. Man and ghost could seem to confront each other. The Polytechnic showed a *Temptations of St. Anthony* in which Anthony was alone on the stage but seemed to be joined at times by seductive spectral tempters hovering about him.

The ghosts shown at the Polytechnic during the 1860s were, by all accounts, awesome, and brought the Polytechnic great popularity. The effect was dubbed "Pepper's Ghost," after Professor John Henry Pepper, director of the Polytechnic during this period.

The effect was also used for a sideshow in which a volunteer spectator was apparently turned into a skeleton. It became a popular feature at magic theatres.

The technical procedures for these illusions had been developed by Henry Dircks, a civil engineer, who in 1864 described the innovation—and his legal claims to it—in a book entitled *The Ghost!* It is significant that Dircks called his invention the "Dircksian Phantasmagoria," reflecting the continuing impact of Robertson's achievement. Similarly, in Paris, the magician Robin referred to his illusions as "Living Phantasmagoria." The term "Phantasmagoria" now became associated with optical effects derived not from slides but from people, who could move.

The Dircksian machinery brought to magic and theatre performances a new rash of the ghostly and macabre. In his book Dircks even gave detailed instructions for staging an apparent on-stage beheading, by ingenious reflections from the "phantom stage" below. Dircks conceded that such entertainment might not be "desirable" but said that "the modus operandi is capable of happier applications."[10] Somehow the happier applications eluded magicians. However one may explain, in psychological terms, the magician's persistent romance with ghouls, there seems little

Raising a ghost by magic lantern—from the book *The Magic Lantern: How To Buy and How To Use It, and How To Raise a Ghost* ("by A Mere Phantom"), 1880   (*Library of Congress*)

Sideshow—man into skeleton

Explanation. A volunteer steps, by invitation, into an upright casket. He is blinded by bright lights facing him. He cannot see the skeleton at the side, which is in darkness. Its position also masks it from him, as well as from the spectators. When the lights on the man are suddenly turned off and the lights on the skeleton turned on at the same moment, the man becomes invisible to the spectators, and they see instead, in the identical position, the reflected image of the skeleton in its casket. The man is aware of the amazement of the audience, but he himself sees nothing. (*Library of Congress*)

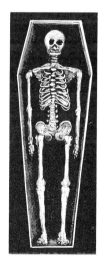

29

doubt that the Robertson and Dircks technologies facilitated and encouraged the trend. It became part of the traditions that magicians would bring to the world of cinema.

Paralleling the Dircksian ghosts, mediums were at this time creating excitement over something similar in effect—"spirit photographs." According to the mediums, sensitive photography could detect spectral presences not visible to the human eye. It could thus show a bereaved person that the spirit of a departed one was still hovering about, keeping watch. The magicians denounced the spirit photographs as charlatanry—mere "double exposures"—and were in turn condemned by the spiritualists. The spirit photographs continued for some time, as did the ar-

Poster of the magician Robin, spectral specialist, 1850s   (*Library of Congress*)

Ghosts, ghosts, and more ghosts   (*Library of Congress*)

gument—a new phase in the continuing struggle between the two groups, so antagonistic yet related.[11]

While the advent of the powerful limelight was inspiring new incursions into the spectre world, it also opened another, quite different career for the magic lantern. Rear projection had been the prevalent procedure not only because it aided secrecy, but also because weak light required a short throw. Front projection from a position near the screen inevitably blocked audience vision. With a powerful light, projection from behind the audience, or even from a booth in back of the auditorium, became feasible.[12] This helped the magic lantern to become the companion of lecturers, an overt presence. Or rather, the magic lantern now embarked on a double life—an overt aide to lecturers, a covert tool for others including magicians and spiritualists.

Illusions for sale: advertisements in the magazine *Mahatma*, 1895

Spirit photograph   (*Library of Congress*)

Magic lantern—illustration from Marion, *L'Optique*, 1874   (*Library of Congress*)

Lantern Adventures

. . . strange things to appear on a wall, very pretty.

—Pepys

Even in its role as aide to lecturers, the magic lantern developed virtuosity during the remaining decades of the century. The possibility of "dissolving"—the cinema term was already in use—from one picture to another, to emphasize contrast or relationship, was well understood. It originally required two lanterns, but the introduction in the 1870s of Keevil's Patent Newtonian Lantern enabled one instrument to show both slides in precisely correct registration, and to dissolve from one to the other or show both simultaneously in superimposition. At the same time slides with movable parts, to be manipulated by lever, proliferated. The bicyclist could move across the landscape, the rocket could zoom to the moon. The saw could saw the tree, and the tree could fall. The periodical *The Magic Lantern*, "a monthly journal of lantern practice" launched in 1875, kept devotees aware of new technical refinements, and of the availability of encyclopedic sets of slides such as "Wilson's Lantern Journeys," and slides for such special purposes as temperance drives and missionary endeavors. One of the missionary sets offered Bible slides with movable elements. Abraham, ready to sacrifice his son, held a dagger in his hand. Hand and dagger could be made to move toward the prostrate Isaac as the story was told. One missionary's experience with such slides was reported with enthusiasm in *The Magic Lantern:*

> The magic lantern produced quite an excitement in Shinte's town. The first picture exhibited was that of Abraham offering

35

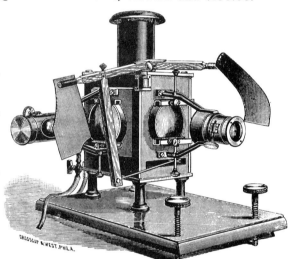
Advertisement in *The Magic Lantern*—arrival of the duplex lantern, 1879

Dissolving views and lantern journeys—advertisement in *The Magic Lantern,* 1879

his son. The picture, large as life, and brought out vividly, produced a great effect, and the story filled their untutored minds with wonder and delight; but when at last the dagger was seen moving toward Isaac, the women were wild with fright, and dashed away, as for life. Shinte himself was charmed, and was deeply interested in examining the apparatus.[13]

But if the magic lantern was becoming a flexible instrument for speakers, it was serving magicians in far more spectacular fashion. Under Georges Méliès, the Théâtre Robert-Houdin specialized in neverland narratives in exotic settings—moonscapes, woodland grottoes, undersea vistas, fires of hell—often combining scenery with projections from many lanterns. Scenes could change from winter to spring to summer to fall. They could be subjected to catastrophic storms, floods, earthquakes, hailstorms. Similarly, at Egyptian Hall, magic effects were often embedded in narratives involving complex projected effects. At the Polytechnic, where the Dircksian Phantasmagoria had begun its career, use could be made of as many as fifteen magic lanterns, operated from a booth that ran the width of the theatre. The future film maker Cecil Hepworth, whose father was on the Polytechnic staff, spent some of his boyhood hours observing the optical trickery there, and it served him "wondrously" in later years.[14]

It was a period of visual novelties and enchantments. In Berlin and Vienna in the 1880s Ottomar Anschütz's Electrical Tachyscope—"electric rapid vision"—entertained people with sequences of leaping horses and gymnastic razzle-dazzle; it was shown at the Chicago World's Fair in 1893. Dioramas and wax museums were popular delights in many cities. The Musée Grévin in Paris, one of the most celebrated wax museums, featured magicians in its Cabinet Fantastique—a small theatre. In 1892 it became the home of Émile Reynaud's Théâtre Optique, which presented fanciful stories in a primitive form of cartoon animation.

Amid all this visual extravaganza, it is not surprising that magicians—along with other showmen—were alert to news and rumor about a new wonder that, it was widely expected, would top all others, or that its debut in December 1895 under the name Cinématographe set off a gold rush. The frenzy of that rush was heightened by a special set of circumstances: the earlier arrival of the peepshow Kinetoscope, and the legal anomalies surrounding it.

Anschütz's Electrical Tachyscope—as portrayed in *Scientific American*, 1889 (*Library of Congress*)

Reynaud's Optical Theatre—as portrayed in *Scientific American*, 1892 (*Library of Congress*)

Peep into Things To Come

Nought may endure but Mutability.
　　　　　　　　　—Shelley

The Kinetoscope, product of Thomas Edison and his co-workers, particularly William Kennedy Laurie Dickson, made its debut in 1894—the year before the debut of the Cinématographe. The two events were closely related. The Kinetoscope made "living pictures" a reality for peepshow visitors. At the same time the images provided a view of what was sure to come. It was at once clear that the mechanism could be combined with a magic lantern to serve audiences as well as individuals. Numerous experimenters began to work toward that next step.

Even as a peepshow, living pictures had extraordinary impact and drew floods of coins. As orders for machines poured in, they soon reached every continent—along with an unknown number of counterfeit Kinetoscopes.[15]

Among those who made unauthorized Kinetoscopes was a respected British optical instrument maker, Robert W. Paul. He was visited by two Greek entrepreneurs, George Georgiades and George Trajedis, who had bought Edison Kinetoscope equipment but wished to expand their activity as quickly as possible and wanted Paul to make machines for them. He demurred at first, but on discovering that Edison had neglected to patent his invention internationally, he accepted the order. During 1894-95 he fabricated more than sixty peepshow machines, adding some improvements of his own. Meanwhile he began experiments toward the next step, a "projecting Kinetoscope." During 1895, while

Kinetoscope (and phonograph) parlor, Detroit, 1894. This was managed by Charles Urban, later a leading figure in the British film world. (*National Film Archive, London*)

working to perfect this invention—the Theatrograph, he called it—he held private previews, to enthusiastic approval.

Edison, though he had not patented his Kinetoscope, was copyrighting films he made for use in the machines. Paul tried to obtain Edison films to show in his own unauthorized machines, but was rebuffed by Edison. Paul, to pursue his work, felt he had to go into the making of films, and he developed a camera for the purpose.[16]

His activities were paralleled by other experimenters in various countries—in France, by Louis Lumière; in the United States, by Thomas Armat, C. Francis Jenkins, and the Latham brothers, Gray and Otway; in England, by Birt Acres, who worked briefly with Paul in production activities; and in Germany by Max Skladanowski and Oskar Messter. *

The race of the inventors was won by Louis Lumière. During one night of insomnia in December 1894 he apparently glimpsed

Robert W. Paul (*National Film Archive, London*)

solutions to all the technical problems, and the making of a prototype followed quickly. He too held private previews, while training *opérateurs* for international exploitation tours. By the end of 1895 some twenty Cinématographe machines were ready—projectors which could also serve as cameras or printing machines. On the tours, each *opérateur* would be able to demonstrate the wonder and make new films en route. On December 28, 1895, the invention was given its historic première at the Grand Café in Paris. This became the signal for a chaotic scramble, a rush for wealth and glory, in which numerous magicians took part.

* The Messter family, like Robert Paul, was in the optical instrument business, serving the medical profession with microscopes, ophthalmoscopes, and laryngoscopes, and was occasionally asked by magicians to make equipment for optical illusions. The clients had included the celebrated magician Bellachini. Both sides always wanted such arrangements kept secret, but the involvement drew Oskar Messter increasingly into projection experiments. Thus the "father of German cinema" came into the film world by a route similar to that of Robert W. Paul, considered by many the "father of British cinema." See Messter, *Mein Weg mit dem Film.*

The Scramble

He comes, the herald of a noisy world.

—Cowper

Georges Méliès

Born in 1861, Georges Méliès was the son of a prosperous shoe manufacturer. Along with two elder brothers, he was expected to carry on the family business and was trained for it.[17] Georges seems to have been the only brother who resisted the role planned for him. The training included a year of retail selling in London—in a shoe store and a corset shop. During this time he became a habitué of Egyptian Hall, whose magic shows presented no language barriers to the young Frenchman. By the time he left London he was a magic addict, constantly practicing prestidigitation. In Paris he took lessons from Émile Voisin, who owned a shop selling magic equipment. Voisin did business with various establishments offering magic, including the Grévin wax museum, and obtained for Méliès his first appearance there at its Cabinet Fantastique, as well as appearances elsewhere. Meanwhile Méliès drew occasional political cartoons under the pseudonym Geo. Smile. And he supervised equipment at the family factory, probably reinforcing his technical skills.

In 1888, when the elder Méliès had retired and decided to cede the business to his three sons, Georges promptly sold his share to his brothers. That year the Théâtre Robert-Houdin was offered for sale by the widow of Robert-Houdin's son, and the twenty-seven-year-old magic addict was able to buy it, thanks to the rev-

Georges Méliès (*National Film Archive, London*)

enue from the sale of his share. The theatre was in decline, but Méliès was determined to rejuvenate it. He became a skillful producer of imaginative sketches combining the romantic, spectacular, and absurd—"genre féerique et fantasmagorique," Méliès called it, suggesting a lingering persistence of the Robertson tradition.

Méliès was aware of the experiments being conducted by Lumière. These made use of rented quarters above the Théâtre Robert-Houdin, and Méliès, who must have known something of what was going on, awaited the première with keen interest. As told later by Méliès, his efforts after the première to buy a machine for the Théâtre Robert-Houdin were rebuffed by the Lumières, and Méliès had to turn elsewhere.[18]

Apparently he knew, or soon learned, where to turn. His mistress, the actress Jehanne D'Alcy—who later became the second Mme. Méliès—had been touring England, and had seen experiments of Robert W. Paul. She told Méliès enthusiastically about Paul's work.[19] The information she provided prompted Méliès to make two trips to London, one in February and another in March, 1896. These trips enabled Méliès to make living pictures a regular part of the Robert-Houdin programs starting April 8, using Paul projectors and films provided by Paul. Meanwhile, studying the projectors, Méliès was able to design a motion picture camera, and had it fabricated by a mechanic. Thus, only a few months after the debut of the Cinématographe, Méliès succeeded in plunging into a film-making career that would eventually account for some five hundred films. At the Robert-Houdin the new feature, which Paul had named the Theatrograph, became the Méliès Kinétograph. From the start, Méliès looked on his films as

Genre féerique et fantasmagorique—Méliès design for *The Palace of the Arabian Nights*, filmed in 1905   (*Library of Congress*)

magic items to enrich the programs of the Robert-Houdin, while earning additional revenue through sale to other establishments. His magic theatre remained the center of his life, but it also became the wellspring of a flood of films, including some of the most imaginative of pioneer films.

Emile and Vincent Isola

Other magicians besides Méliès witnessed the miracle of the Cinématographe at the Grand Café and were determined to acquire it. The extraordinary Isola brothers, like Méliès, would not take no for an answer.

The Isolas had been born and raised in Algeria.[20] Their father, who ran a small shop there, was the illegitimate son of an Italian countess who had left Italy to have her baby. The countess's grandsons, Émile and Vincent, grew up on the edge of poverty but received machine-shop training, while they dreamed of careers as magicians and studied every magician who came to Algeria. The legend of Robert-Houdin's exploits in Algiers held special fascination for them. In 1880, as teenagers, they used their first earnings to head for Paris—for machine-shop work and, when they could manage it, evenings at the Robert-Houdin. Along with long hours in a railway repair shop they began giving magic performances in cafés and clubs. Growing acclaim led to an engagement for a magic act in the Folies Bergère, where they were so successful that in 1892 they were able to launch their own magic theatre, the Théâtre Isola, in competition with the Robert-Houdin. They soon became the wonder boys of Paris and eventually bought and directed the Folies Bergère,[21] while also managing other theatres including the Sarah Bernhardt. But in 1895 they were intent on new magic for the Théâtre Isola and, like Méliès and others, were at the Grand Café and, when rebuffed, turned elsewhere—perhaps to Robert Paul. Or perhaps the Isolatograph, with which they began film showings at the Théâtre Isola on April 8—four days after the first Méliès film show—was a product of their own technical ingenuity. In any case, the Isolas embarked not only on the showing of films but on the manufacture and sale of projectors. Within weeks of their own debut they sold Isolatographs for use in Berlin, Vienna, Brussels, Moscow. So hectic was the pace of events that Berlin's

Jehanne D'Alcy   (*Museum of Modern Art, New York*)

The Isolatograph of the Isola brothers (*Deutsches Museum, Munich*)

first film theatre, at Unter den Linden 21, opened that same month—April 1896—with an Isolatograph projector.[22]

Félicien Trewey

Why did Louis Lumière, after the triumphant Cinématographe debut in Paris—it was soon running at three locations there—entrust the all-important London opening to his friend Félicien Trewey, a magician?

Watching the astonishment at the Grand Café, did he himself perhaps see the Cinématographe not as a "communication" instrument but as a new wonder like the Dircksian Phantasmagoria—something that would amaze people for a few years and then gradually fade away? Some of the comments ascribed to the Lumières, and their plans for whirlwind exploitation under careful control, suggest such an attitude. In any case, the Cinématographe arrived in England under the supervision of the magician Félicien Trewey. The show was advertised as "under the management of Mons. Trewey" or sometimes "under the personal direction of Monsieur Trewey." It was unveiled at the Polytechnic, home of optical wonders, in showings that were in the nature of demonstrations for royalty and show-business impresa-

50

POLYTECHNIC.

LUMIÈRE
CINEMATOGRAPHE

1. The Landing Stage

2. Boating

3. Place des Cordeliers   (Lyon)

4. The Biter Bit

5. Arrival of a Train in a Country Station

6. Practical Joke on the Gardener

7. Babies Playing

8. Fall of a Wall

9. Trewey's "Under the Hat"

10. Bathing in the Mediterranean.

Under the management of Mons. TREWEY.

ORIGINALITY not IMITATION.

Lecturer   FRANCIS POCHET

Trewey's program at the Polytechnic   (*National Film Archive, London*)

51

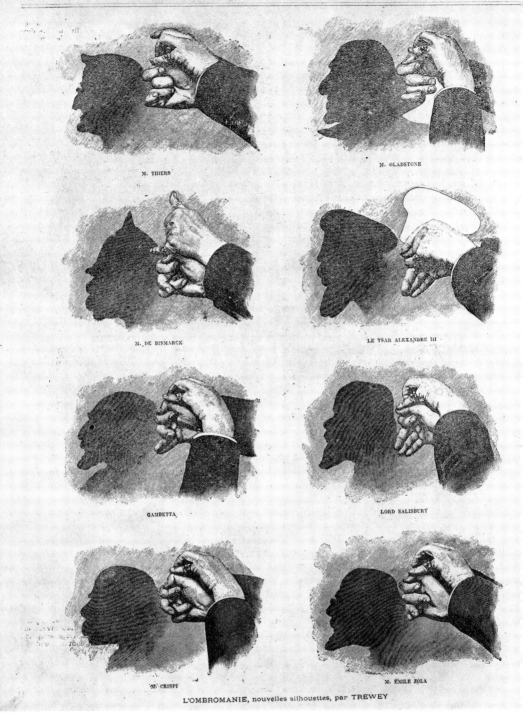

M. THIERS

M. GLADSTONE

M. DE BISMARCK

LE TSAR ALEXANDRE III

GAMBETTA

LORD SALISBURY

M. CRISPI

M. ÉMILE ZOLA

L'OMBROMANIE, nouvelles silhouettes, par TREWEY

Silhouettes by Trewey—a page from the magic magazine *Mahatma,*
October 1895   (*Library of Congress*)

rios. These limited previews began February 20, with later exhibition plans still uncertain.

Trewey was a great name in magic. Born in 1848 in Angoulème, France, he had been sent to a Jesuit school to be trained for the priesthood but had run away. Joining a traveling troupe of jugglers and conjurers, he had acquired skill in virtually all branches of legerdemain. Eventually he became most famous for his virtuosity as *ombromane* or shadowgraphist, telling witty and charming stories while his hands, working in the beam of a magic lantern and manipulating small props, created spellbinding dramas on a screen. He could define a number of characters in vivid detail, returning with precision to each as he led them through moods, actions, and dramatic conflicts. Shadowgraphy, an art of ancient origin, had won new vogue during the nineteenth century, starting in Italy and spreading throughout Europe.[23] Trewey was considered its outstanding master, and he had performed on all continents. He was ready to retire at the time the Cinématographe was invented, but Louis Lumière persuaded him to introduce it into England. Trewey had always had great success there. And perhaps he and Lumière both saw the Cinématographe as the ultimate development of shadowgraphy. Certainly shadowgraphy can be seen as a precursor of cinema. As John Barnes of the Barnes Museum of Cinematography has

A frame from *Partie d'écarte* (Card Party), filmed at La Ciotat by Louis Lumière. At the table: Antoine Lumière, father of Louis; Félicien Trewey; their friend Winkler. Louis Lumière's valet looks on. (*National Film Archive, London*)

suggested, its form is echoed in early animated films, as in the early silhouette cartoons of Felix the Cat and the silhouette films of Lotte Reiniger.[24]

With the Cinématographe arriving in Britain under the auspices of a magician, it is not surprising that other magicians flocked to see it, and soon converged on Monsieur Trewey, clamoring for a chance to buy.

David Devant

The dapper David Devant, born in 1868, had become one of the most popular conjurers at Egyptian Hall. It was a matter of course that he attended the previews at the Polytechnic, and he was entranced by what he saw. It seemed to him the key to triumphs at Egyptian Hall. Himself a celebrated shadowgraphist and exponent of diverse optical illusions, he at once went to Trewey as a confrère, hoping to buy. The word he received from Trewey dismayed him. Cinématographe equipment was not for sale. The new wonder could only be booked with authorized Lumière personnel at £100 a week—a steep fee that the Empire Theatre, a large variety hall, had accepted. The Trewey presentation would move there March 9—for a long run, if the Paris experience was an indication.

Devant was devastated. The £100 fee was beyond possibility for the small theatre at Egyptian Hall, which in any case relied on its own miracles. John Nevil Maskelyne, surviving founder of Egyptian Hall and its director, was uninterested in pursuing the matter. Devant could not believe his misfortune.

At home, as he paged through the trade journal *The English Mechanic*, a news item caught his eye. It concerned one Robert W. Paul and his experiments with a projecting Kinetoscope. Paul had apparently given a demonstration at Finsbury Technical College on February 20, the very day of Trewey's arrival at the Polytechnic.

Devant's fevered reaction is described in his memoir, *My Magic Life*.

> My wife and I were about to commence dinner, but on her advice I left the meal and made my way in a hansom cab as quickly as possible to the office of the paper, and there obtained the information that Mr. Paul was a scientific instrument maker

David Devant poster for *The Birth of Flora*, an illusion introduced in the spring of 1895   (*Library of Congress*)

> with a place of business in Hatton Garden. Going to Hatton
> Garden, I found a gentleman just getting into a cab loaded with
> boxes. Here was the inventor I was in search of.
>
> I quickly made my business known and asked for particulars of
> the machine. Mr. Paul told me he was just going to show the in-
> strument at the Olympia at a side-show, and invited me to ac-
> company him there and see it. My time was limited, as I had to
> be back at the Egyptian Hall for the evening show, but after-
> wards would have been too late. I decided to go.[25]

En route, no time was wasted. They discussed an arrangement.
Paul was clearly nervous about his own situation. He had held
successful demonstrations but had not begun commercial exploitation. Now, with the huge acclaim at the Polytechnic, it seemed
that events might pass him by. Paul at the moment had only one
Theatrograph, but he was now determined to make others as
quickly as he could. He would be glad to sell one to David Devant
for £100. He "promised me the first one if I wished, also a com-
mission on any further machines I might be the means of selling." Devant saw the Olympia showing and made up his mind.

The result was that only a few weeks later, on March 19,
1896—ten days after Trewey's Empire Theatre première—David
Devant began showing "animated photographs" as part of his act
at Egyptian Hall. A week later, March 26, another Paul projector
went into action at the Alhambra as part of its variety program,
in which the attraction was renamed the Animatographe. Film
suddenly dominated Devant's life, as well as Paul's. Within
weeks Devant sold additional projectors to magicians—the first
one to an American illusionist, Carl Hertz, who would carry it
far and wide, and two to Georges Méliès, whose quest brought
him to England during these weeks. The Devant-Paul arrangement expanded into film production. In June, Paul shot four
films of Devant doing tricks—with rabbits (*The Mysterious Rabbit*), with eggs (*The Egg-Laying Man*), with shadowgraphy (*Devant's Hand Shadows*), and with paper (*Devant's Exhibition of
Paper Folding*). The films were offered for sale to magic theatres
and other entertainment halls, with Devant again serving as com-
mission agent. Egyptian Hall won a surge of business with "animated photographs," so Maskelyne and Devant began film making
on the roof of Egyptian Hall to keep the shows going. Soon they
were organizing traveling units to tour the provinces with their
"animated photographs" and other magic, using additional pro-

Egyptian Hall poster—introducing Nevil Maskelyne's Mutagraph, patented 1897. It proved less durable than the Robert Paul projectors. (*The Museum of London*)

jectors bought from Paul. John Nevil Maskelyne, now completely enthusiastic, made Devant a partner, along with Nevil Maskelyne, son of the co-founder. Nevil Maskelyne began experiments to develop a projector of his own, the Mutagraph, featuring continuous instead of intermittent motion. It was patented in 1897. He also experimented with high-speed photography for slow-motion effects. As a curious by-product of this new expertise, Nevil Maskelyne was later enlisted by Britain's War Office to document on film the behavior of artillery shells in flight, and he did so successfully.[26]

As Méliès in France stepped up his activities, Devant became the exclusive agent in Britain for the sale of Méliès films—which Méliès called Star Films—as well as equipment made by Méliès.

Through Devant, Paul had suddenly become a busy supplier of film equipment, much of which was going to magicians. As a result of his early demonstrations, Paul said later, "an extraordinary demand arose, first from conjurers" and then from other types of showmen.[27] The seekers came from all over the world, clamoring for projectors and films. On the spiral staircase leading up to Paul's workshop they waited, day and night.

The first of the seekers, the American Carl Hertz, became especially significant. He arrived in Britain in March 1896 for a brief stopover, on the eve of a world tour that would take him to Africa, Asia, and Australia. In London he went first to see the Cinématographe—then, in haste, to Trewey, Paul, Devant.

Carl Hertz

Born in San Francisco about 1859, Carl Hertz was the son of a Russian father and Polish mother who had gone to California in the 1849 gold rush, had not found gold, and had settled down to run a dry-goods store. Carl Hertz grew up knowing a lot about the dry-goods business but constantly practicing magic tricks, trying them out on fellow clerks and willing customers. He gave occasional public performances, not always successfully. But in 1884, while working in Kansas City at the Boston One Price Clothing Store, he got a trial engagement at a local theatre that proved a breakthrough. Clerks from the Boston One Price Clothing Store came in numbers to cheer him on, the engagement was extended, and he made the transition to a career in magic.[28] A decade of constant touring, including an engagement at the Folies Bergère, made him one of the best-known magicians in the world. He was known as an "illusionist" and a flamboyant performer.

He traveled with assistants and many boxes of equipment and a female co-performer, Mademoiselle D'Alton, his Vanishing Lady. Every leading magician at this time had a Vanishing Lady. When hiring Mlle. D'Alton, Hertz had her swear a loyalty oath, since she would know his secrets. His memoirs describe the beginning of their relationship:

> The oath was duly administered, and the contract signed, and thus Emelie D'Alton became the original Vanishing Lady, and, a little later, to make my secrets more secure, she became Mrs. Carl Hertz.[29]

One of their specialties, The Phoenix Illusion, harked back to Robertson's *Fantasmagorie*. Mlle. D'Alton was a heroine condemned to death and consigned to a fiery furnace. Amid billows of smoke and flashes of red, the audience apparently saw her sink in the flames. A large urn was then brought in. Ashes from the furnace were placed in the urn. After suitable incantations, Mlle. D'Alton rose in glory from her ashes.

In Borneo, during an early world tour, Hertz improvised a variation to solve a crisis. A performance before a native potentate, whose daughter sat at her father's feet, was so admired—especially by the daughter, the princess—that the potentate requested several repeat performances. After the second he announced that his daughter had decided to marry Hertz; the ruler himself would officiate the next day, after the performance. Hertz explained that he already had a wife, but this was not considered an obstacle; the princess said she would accept Emelie D'Alton as her equal. Next day, as told in Hertz's memoirs, *A Modern Mystery Merchant*, the company decided to reschedule the Phoenix Illusion, with variations. At the crucial moment Hertz brushed Mlle. D'Alton aside and himself plunged into the fiery furnace. Later, amid horror and dismay, it was explained that something had gone wrong. The ashes were not working. Mourning replaced festivity as Hertz's aides carried him from the area in a wicker basket loaded with equipment.[30]

In March 1896 Carl Hertz, an enthusiastic exponent of scientific magic, saw the Cinématographe at once as the ultimate illusion. In a few days he would sail for Africa and was determined to include it in his tour. Trewey gave his usual answer. Devant was willing to sell him a Paul machine but had none available. The existing equipment was in daily use at Egyptian Hall and the Alhambra, with only one reserve projector on hand— kept at the Alhambra for emergencies. Paul would not part with it, but would make him another, if Hertz could wait. Hertz could not wait. He was to sail in a few days, on March 28.

The day before his sailing, Hertz invited Paul to dinner and made a final effort to persuade Paul to sell him the reserve set. Paul was adamant. Finally Hertz, according to his memoirs, said: "Well, you had better take me over to the Alhambra and explain to me the working of the machine and all about it, so that I shall understand how to use it when one is sent out to me." The account continues:

> So we went to the Alhambra, where he took me to the stage and showed me the whole working of the machine—how to fix the films in and everything concerning it. We were there for over an hour, during which I kept pressing him to let me have one of the

machines. Finally I said: "Look here! I am going to take one of these machines with me now." With that I took out £100 in notes, put them into his hand, got a screwdriver, and almost before he knew it, I had one of the machines unscrewed from the floor of the stage and onto a four-wheeler. The next day I sailed for South Africa on the Norman. . . .[31]

A few days later on the S.S. *Norman*, Carl Hertz presented what must have been the first film showing on any ocean liner. And on May 9, 1896, in the Empire Theatre of Johannesburg, South Africans saw their first motion picture as part of Hertz's magic show. The films proved a "fantastic draw"—so much so, that Hertz had a problem. He had brought only five short films provided by Paul. He sent cables to London pleading for more, but saw little hope of getting them in time. Then, in an arcade, he noticed a sign:

KINETOSCOPE: ADMISSION SIXPENCE

The proprietor of the Kinetoscope establishment had a badly worn supply of Edison films which he was apparently willing to sell. He parted with twenty of them for £10—perhaps sensing that Hertz's new feature would doom his Kinetoscope peepshow parlor. But the purchase confronted Hertz with a new problem. Finding that the sprocket holes of the Kinetoscope films were different from those of his other films, he spent days cementing tiny bits of film over the Edison sprocket holes, then making new sprocket holes to fit his own equipment.

The African visit was a triumph. Then off to Australia and another première, another triumph. Melbourne Opera House, August 22, 1896: the beginning of film history in Australia.[32]

Hertz went on for runs in other Australian cities, then introduced the motion picture in New Zealand and in various cities of China, Indo-China, India, Burma, Ceylon. His journeys crisscrossed those of other entrepreneurs. A Lumière *opérateur* beat him to Bombay, but Hertz had already beaten him to Australia. Along with Hertz, other magic acts were descending on India with cinematographic marvels; the arrivals included a "Hughes Photo-Motoscope" and "Professor Anderson and Mlle. Blanche and their Andersonoscopograph."[33]

Everywhere, amazement. Hertz returned to Australia for a second tour, and was reported to have cleared £10,000 in Australia

Carl Hertz poster—return visit to Australia, 1898 (*Library of Congress*)

alone—an extraordinary amount for the time.[34] Yet his experience had a sobering aspect. In spite of the spectacular nature of some of Hertz's magic, there seemed no question that the film items had become the main attraction. Hertz's own references to film as a "fantastic draw" make this clear. And the film historian Mervyn Wasson, in *The Beginning of Film in Australia*, writes of Hertz's first Melbourne run:

> People returned night after night to whistle a second before a gentleman in the film of Westminster Bridge turned to look at the cameraman, a game that gave endless amusement.[35]

Some of the theatres and other entertainment places where magicians unveiled the wonder in 1896 would soon turn into cinema halls. Jay Leyda in *Dianying* mentions a Shanghai tea garden that in 1897 offered a program of Edison films which it announced as "entirely mechanized."[36]

Professor Anderson

The Professor Anderson whose path crossed Carl Hertz's in India was apparently Phillip Anderson, who toured South Asian countries through the 1880s and 1890s. He toured with his first wife and later with a second wife, Blanche de la Cour or "Mlle. Blanche." Many people thought the "Professor" was the great John Henry Anderson, "Wizard of the North," one of the most charismatic figures in magic history. Phillip Anderson, imitating the wizard's performance, permitted the impression to exist or sometimes said he was Anderson's son. It is thought likely he was a former assistant of John Henry Anderson.[37] The Wizard of the North had died in 1874.

The Andersonoscopograph may have been one more incarnation of Robert Paul's projector, which acquired a new name from each of its many buyers. But other sources were increasingly available.

Leopoldo Fregoli

Late in 1897 Louis Lumière abandoned his policy of not selling Cinématographes. He would henceforth sell to anyone who cared to buy. At the same time he would give up the exploitation and

Bioscope, Electrograph, Eknetographe, Kinematographe, Eidoloscope, Thaumatographe, Ikonograph, Actograph, Cameragraphe, Biactograph, Polyscope, Scenematographe, Andersonoscopographe, Photo-Motoscope, Fregoligraph, *et al.* (*National Film Archive, London*)

production tours through which his *opérateurs* had in two years introduced the invention on every continent and planted the word *cinema* into most of the world's languages.

The paths of his *opérateurs* had criss-crossed those of magicians and other showmen. The growing number and diversity of such showmen, and the proliferation of imitation equipment, may have influenced the Lumière policy shift, or at least its timing. The Lumières were most at home in the devising and manufacture of equipment, and this would now be their domain. The Lumière decision probably drove a number of marginal products off the market.

One of the first to buy a Cinématographe from the Lumières was the Italian magician Leopoldo Fregoli. Louis Lumière, a Fregoli admirer, invited him to Lyon for a technical orientation. Fregoli spent every day for a month at the Lumière plant.[38]

Born in Rome in 1867, Fregoli was a prodigy who early in life astonished audiences with his ability to transform face and voice into scores of different characters. A warm wit and uproarious gift for mimicry won him a growing vogue. Meanwhile he acquired the skills of a conjurer, and the combination enabled him to perform sketches in which he played a dozen or more distinct characters, making instantaneous transformations—in details of clothing and accouterments as well as voice, face, height, girth, posture—that completely baffled observers. He sometimes performed an entire trial, playing judge, defendant, attorneys, witnesses, and members of the jury. Few magicians have been praised in more extravagant terms than Fregoli. The French called him a *transformiste*.

Completing his orientation in Lyon, Fregoli renamed his new attraction the Fregoligraph and began to make short films, which he featured in his stage performances. Many of these were filmed versions of vignettes he had previously done on the stage. They were offered for sale; some appeared in Robert W. Paul catalogues. But Fregoli, along with others, readily grasped the possibilities of film trickery, such as reversals. In one filmed sketch he was seen carefully dressing, after which his clothes suddenly flew off, resuming their place on the chair. He also saw that film had its own possibilities for transformations. In *The Lightning Change Artist*, made for Méliès in 1899, he appeared as twenty different characters—his usual specialty—but tried to make the transformations even more baffling by making cuts between segments. In other words, he filmed separate segments and spliced them together.[39]

Judging by the speed with which such works were imitated, they must have won considerable early success. But Fregoli must have seen that what he was doing did not require the skills of a *transformiste* or any other kind of magician. Reasonably accomplished film technicians could accomplish such transformations, and were doing so. Fregoli's films were soon engulfed by similar trick films, which must also have made his stage performances less amazing. Fregoli's situation epitomized the problems of the magician in the strange new world of living pictures.

Alexander the Great

Among those who flocked to buy the Lumière Cinématographe was Alexander Victor, who as a magician adopted the name—the choice must have been irresistible—Alexander the Great. He had been born in 1878 in the small lumbering town of Bollnas in northern Sweden. His father was a military man, often moving from place to place, so that the boy was exposed to a variety of schooling and experience. He seems to have been a prize pupil in physics.

In 1894, at sixteen, he attended a performance of the magician The Great Stephanio, as a result of which he acquired a consuming interest in the inventing of mechanical illusions. He offered himself to Stephanio as a technical assistant and was hired. Tours with The Great Stephanio eventually took him to Paris, where they saw an early performance of the Cinématographe. Later, according to Victor's reminiscences, they were able to buy a Lumière machine and a selection of films, and the attraction proved a sensation.[40] When Stephanio died in Cairo while on tour, Victor was able to carry on with the act largely because of the films. But he learned other optical illusions, like walking through solid walls. As Alexander the Great he made appearances in various Asian and European cities before migrating to the United States late in the 1890s. There his magic tours—including film—alternated with excursions into other enterprises. Terry Ramsaye in *A Million and One Nights* credits him with opening an early store-front theatre in Newark, N.J.[41] But a more important development came from a disaster that struck him in Toledo, Ohio, and which is detailed by David H. Shepard in *The Victor Animato-graph Company.*

When a theatre refused to make a trap door needed by Victor for one of his illusions, he moved his scenery and equipment to a warehouse to await his next engagement. Then the warehouse burned down. Stranded, Victor turned salesman for the White Lily Washing Machine Company of Davenport, Iowa, for which he soon afterwards invented an electric washing machine—which brought him back to the inventing business, as well as to film. An article in the *Toledo Times* for February 2, 1910, quoted by Shepard, refers to a Victor motion picture invention called the Animato-Graph, and also to Victor's experiments in "television"— which the article describes as the art of showing pictures or scenes by telephone or telegraph.

The Animatograph—as the invention came to be spelled—was a film system designed for home use. A company to exploit it was founded in Davenport in 1910, with $100,000 in financial back-ing from the White Lily Washing Machine Company, which was clearly impressed with Victor and his invention. The Davenport *Daily Times* of June 17, 1910, said it "promises to revolutionize the motion picture business . . . as it will enable any person to take the motion pictures, develop and print them, and reproduce them on a screen in a simple manner and at small cost. It gives promise of making the motion picture machine as common and as popular in the home as the graphophone."

The prediction was on target. The company turned out to be the birthplace of the non-theatrical film industry, which after long struggles standardized on 16mm, and flourished. The chief architect—of the company and of the industry—was the magi-cian Alexander the Great, who here abandoned the magician's obsession with secrecy and resolved to make an invention avail-able to one and all.

He lived to be eighty-two, still working on inventions. But at his home in California he liked to invite children in for a bit of magic, which he performed with trembling hands.[42]

Walter R. Booth

The magician Walter R. Booth was drawn into the new film magic by Robert W. Paul, as Paul's first film-making efforts widened into steady production.

Paul, more than anyone else, is felt to deserve the title "father

Alexander the Great—inventor. In this 1944 photograph Alexander Victor poses with an early Animatograph (model 2) and his latest sound projector. (*Victor Animatograph Collection, University of Iowa*)

of British cinema."[43] His inquisitiveness and restless energy drove him into every aspect of film: invention, manufacture, exhibition, distribution, film production. Since his first film successes involved magicians, it is not surprising that he enlisted a magician to aid his film-making. Booth headed Paul's film production activities until 1906. "With the valuable aid of Walter Booth and others," Paul later recounted, "hundreds of humorous, dramatic, and trick films were produced in the studio."[44]

In this flood of films, some were magic acts on film, not unlike Paul's first films of Devant. *The Hindoo Juggler* (1900), in which a juggler was seen passing swords through a boy in a basket, was typical of this sort. Others exhibited the fanciful imagination and zany humor that also characterized Méliès. They were essentially Booth films, with Paul serving as entrepreneur—executive producer and distributor.

In one early Paul-Booth film, *An Overincubated Baby* (1901), a baby is placed in a professor's incubator—apparently for too long. He comes out an old man.

A longer film, *The Motorist,* probably made in 1905, is characteristic of the later, more ambitious work. A motorist, pursued by a policeman, escapes by zooming off into space. After circling the sun he takes a ride around the rings of Saturn, then starts falling back toward earth. He crashes through a roof, landing in what turns out to be a courthouse. As the forces of law move in to arrest him, the auto suddenly changes into a horse-drawn cart, which proceeds out of the courtroom. When out of the reach of the law, it changes back into an automobile and makes good its escape.

In 1906 Booth moved to the Urban Trading Company. Here he made what has been called Britain's first animated film, *The Hand of the Artist* (1906). He remained active as a film maker for many years.

Charles Urban, Detroit Kinetoscope parlor operator in 1894, moved to London as Edison representative and soon became a leading figure of the British film world. In 1900 he succeeded David Devant as exclusive British agent for films of Georges Méliès. For Urban, Booth made *The Hand of the Artist* (1906), described as Britain's "first animated cartoon." (*National Film Archive, London*)

The Motorist, 1905—by Walter R. Booth for Robert W. Paul. In 1906 Booth went to work for the Urban Trading Company—see opposite. (*National Film Archive, London*)

G. W. Bitzer

G. Wilhelm Bitzer—"Billy" Bitzer—was born in 1872 in Roxbury, Massachusetts. Many in the Bitzer family were silversmiths. Billy was expected to carry on the tradition, and started in that direction, working up to a job at Gorham's, where he earned the substantial sum of $25 a week. But another interest intervened.

He had long been obsessed with magic. At home he had constantly practiced magic tricks, especially when he could persuade his sister Anna to serve as assistant or audience or whatever was needed. On an apartment house roof he had contrived a photo of her "seeming to walk a tightrope—my first bit of trick photography." The fact that she was "fat" apparently gave the photo added piquancy.[45]

In 1894, at the age of twenty-two, he was offered a job at $12 a week in the Magic Introduction Company, a New York concern with upstairs offices selling magic equipment and technical novelties. It meant cutting his earnings in half, but he could not resist the chance to work with all that magic gadgetry. It seemed an "open sesame" to a new world of wonder, the key to a new career. And it turned out to be that.

The owner of the Magic Introduction Company, Elias Bernard Koopman, was getting interested in a new kind of magic equipment. William Kennedy Laurie Dickson, who had played a central role in the inventing of Edison's Kinetoscope but had left Edison, persuaded Koopman and other entrepreneurs to finance the development of a rival peepshow machine, the Mutoscope. Working on a different principle, it was really a mechanized flip-card device. A sequence of photos mounted on a wheel was flipped into position in rapid order as the wheel was turned, providing a vivid illusion of motion. The American Mutoscope Company began business in 1895 on the premises of the Magic Introduction Company, and Bitzer soon got the assignment of photographing flip-card novelties for the machine, such as *Little Egypt* (a belly dancer or "serpentine" dancer), *How Girls Go to Bed*, and *How Girls Undress*.[46]

Within months it became clear that the future belonged not to peepshows in penny arcades but to projected images in theatres, and the company worked at frenzied pace to develop its own projection machine, the Biograph. Unveiled to New York audiences

Flip-card book (*Collection of Kemp R. Niver and J. P. Niver*)

Mutoscope viewing machine (*Collection of Kemp R. Niver and J. P. Niver*)

on October 12, 1896 at Hammerstein's Olympia Music Hall—after trials elsewhere—it won instant and resounding success. The Mutoscope Company evolved into the Mutoscope and Biograph Company and eventually into Biograph, most astonishing of early studios. One of Bitzer's first Biograph assignments was to help Dickson photograph (or "biograph") Republican presidential candidate William McKinley at Canton, Ohio, where the latter was conducting his "front-porch" campaign. But as the vogue for trick films gathered momentum, they inevitably became a Bitzer specialty. In this genre he produced a number of remarkably creative items before becoming chief cameraman for the most illustrious figure to emerge from Biograph, D. W. Griffith.

Albert E. Smith and J. Stuart Blackton

Both Albert E. Smith and J. Stuart Blackton were born in England in 1875. Both came to the United States with their families in the immigration surge of the 1880s. As teenagers in New York, both earned a living at odd jobs. Both dreamed of show business. They met each other in 1894 and formed a magic act. Both were nineteen. Another young Englishman, Ronald Reader, joined them in the venture.[47]

In their promotional literature Reader was called a "prestidigitateur." Smith was referred to as an "illusionist"; his magic involved technical gadgetry. He was later described by Terry Ramsaye in *A Million and One Nights* as a "spirit cabinet performer."[48] J. Stuart Blackton joined them as chalk-talk specialist. Possessed of a remarkable talent for rapid sketching, he was getting intermittent assignments from the *New York World* as a freelance reporter, doing stories illustrated with his own sketches. The magic group's promotion proclaimed him "The Komical Kartoonist."

The act had a creaky start. The first audience, in Haverstraw, N.Y., is said to have consisted of two people. Reader soon left the act, but Smith and Blackton persevered. In July 1895 they were talking of buying a magic lantern to help create a Rip Van Winkle sequence when they came on a Kinetoscope parlor on Nassau Street in downtown New York, which pulled them up sharp. "All

Brochure for a magic act: the Reader, Smith and Blackton combination—embryo of the American Vitagraph Company, which metamorphosed into Warner Brothers (*Courtesy Anthony Slide*)

we have to do," said Blackton, "is invent a machine which will project on a sheet enlarged reproductions of the little moving pictures we see in the Kinetoscope." Smith, the official machinist of the act, was expected to come up with the invention. They soon learned that others had already done so.

Within months they were reading about the Lumière Cinématographe, as well as Edison's countermoves with a so-called Edison Vitascope, and other competitive entries with Greek-sounding and Latin-sounding names: Polyscope, Phantascope, and innumerable others. Clearly, great events and struggles were in the making. In April 1896 the *New York World* suddenly pushed the magic partners into the midst of those events.

The Evening World wanted Blackton to interview Edison, with sketches, about the Edison Vitascope projector, which had just had its debut at Koster & Bial's Music Hall on 34th Street in New York City. Blackton, clutching his sketchbook, went to New Jersey and appeared at Edison's laboratory office. "Hello young man, what are you doing here?" said Edison. Blackton introduced himself to the deaf inventor in a bellowing voice. Edison said: "All right, you have a good strong voice and I can hear you, young man. Sit down." They talked, while Blackton made a sketch of Edison and then sketches of various national leaders. Apparently Edison took to the Komical Kartoonist. He was delighted with the sketches and wanted to see more. Blackton kept sketching. He was supposed to interview Edison but Edison kept interviewing him.

> Then he asked me if I could draw that picture of him on a big paper on a board. I told him that I could and he said, "You come on out to the Black Maria," and we did and he had them get boards and wide white paper and some charcoal, and right then and there he had the camera recording your humble servant drawing a picture of Thomas A. Edison. He said, "Put your name on that board," and, "This will be a good ad for you. It will go all over the country in the show houses." I did, and that was my entry into the motion picture industry. I finished that picture with the name of Blackton, Cartoonist of the *New York Evening World*, written all over the top of that board.[49]

A more important moment came as they said good-by. Blackton asked if he and Smith might buy an Edison Vitascope for use in their act. Edison dismissed the idea. Vitascope projectors were not sold, he explained; you had to buy rights for a territory. But then he added that he was working on a small machine that would do everything the Vitascope could do, and that it would be on the market in a few months. "It will be called the Edison Projecting Kinetoscope."* Blackton said he would like to order one. Edison, according to Blackton's recollection, "rang the bell for a boy, and I gave the order for a machine." A few months later the machine arrived, along with a few Edison films, for which the partners paid $800. According to Terry Ramsaye, it was No. 13 of the new Edison projector, which Edison was selling to anyone—a policy similar to the new Lumière policy. Smith studied the mechanism, and in a short time designed a camera to make films for it. So the magic partners started production. The idea was to enrich the magic act, but it led to greater things. As film producers, Smith and Blackton turned into the American Vitagraph Company. Formed in 1896, it began business in 1897 and grew with startling rapidity. The mushrooming enterprise gradually submerged the magic act.

In later years Smith made light of his magic prowess. But in February 1899 the magic trade periodical *Mahatma* featured Smith on its cover and described him as a "lyceum prestidigitateur" with "few if any equals." His repertoire, said *Mahatma*, "is distinctly unique and original, being a clever combination of sleight of hand and invisible mechanical appliances of his own invention. . . . A peep into his dark rooms and workshop in the Morse building, New York, would prove an interesting sight to any visiting magician."[50]

But Smith's technical virtuosity was moving in new directions and playing an important role in the rapid rise of Vitagraph. He constantly devised improvements in equipment and applied the same inventiveness to production problems. He records in his

---

* Edison had not invented the Edison Vitascope, which was the work of Thomas Armat and C. Francis Jenkins. Edison, taken off-guard by the success of the Cinématographe, agreed to the release of the Vitascope as the "Edison Vitascope" to maintain his competitive position, but he apparently disliked the arrangement. Although he had a stake in the Edison Vitascope, he was about to challenge its status with an Edison Projecting Kinetoscope.

The only Paper in the United States devoted to the Interests of Magicians, Spiritualists, Mesmerists, Etc.

Vol. II. No. VIII.   NEW YORK, FEBRUARY, 1899.   Single Copy, 10 Cents.

MR. ALBERT E. SMITH, The Popular Lyceum Prestidigitateur.

Albert E. Smith, magician—as featured in *Mahatma,* 1899   (*Library of Congress*)

autobiography, *Two Reels and a Crank,* that in 1899 the papers were full of dramatic accounts of naval action in the Spanish-American War. The theatres were clamoring for films about it; Smith and Blackton decided to make one.

> At this time street vendors in New York were selling sturdy photographs of ships of the American and Spanish fleets. We bought a set of each and we cut out the battleships. On a table, topside down, we placed one of artist Blackton's large canvas-covered frames and filled it with water an inch deep. In order to stand the cutouts in the water, we nailed them to lengths of wood about an inch square. In this way a little "shelf" was provided behind each ship, and on this shelf we placed pinches of gunpowder—three pinches for each ship—not too many, we felt, for a major sea engagement of this sort.[51]

For background Blackton drew white clouds on blue-tinted cardboard. Fine threads were attached to the ships, to guide maneuvers. Smoke was needed, so Mrs. Blackton volunteered to smoke a cigarette, and an office boy said he would try a cigar. Wires, slender enough to escape the eye, were used to touch off the mounds of gunpowder, and the battle was on. Puffing and coughing, Mrs. Blackton delivered a beautiful haze. The explosions were terrifying. Blackton maneuvered the boats, agitated the water, and set off the explosions.

The Battle of Santiago Bay lasted just two minutes. According to Smith's account, film and lenses were sufficiently imperfect to conceal the crudities. It was a smash hit. Magic was giving way to motion picture "special effects."[52]

A few of Vitagraph's early films involved Blackton as cartoonist, and these made contributions to the early history of animation. But Blackton the Komical Kartoonist was rapidly becoming something else—the executive supervising all production at American Vitagraph, a major studio. And the illusionist Albert E. Smith was evolving into the administrative and financial genius of the enterprise, which in due time changed into Warner Brothers, a giant component of a vast industry.

Animation by Blackton: Two frames from *Humorous Phases of Funny Faces*—from the "paper print" copyright deposit, Library of Congress (*David Reese*)

Harry Houdini

Ehrich Weiss, born in Hungary in 1874 and eventually called Houdini, went through many career transitions. He worked as actor, contortionist, and trapezist before turning to magic. As magician he wanted at first to be "like Houdin" and named himself accordingly, emulating some of Robert-Houdin's magic. But again he went through transitions. For a time he was "Houdini, King of Cards" and sometimes "Professor Houdini." The specialty he finally evolved for himself, and through which he reached the peak of fame, made use of all his varied skills—*escapology*, astounding escapes from handcuffs, straitjackets, packing cases, safes, often dangling over city streets or dropped into harbors or rivers. Such feats, done publicly to promote theatre performances, brought fantastic crowds and by the turn of the century were turning him into an international legend.

In 1901, on a European tour, he made a pilgrimage to the Théâtre Robert-Houdin, where a disturbing discovery awaited him: stage magic had vanished from the evening hours in favor of the cinema. Magicians had been relegated to the afternoons. While this troubled Houdini, it also contributed to a new Houdini obsession—to conquer the world of film.[53] That year his first involvement apparently began, in a short Pathé item. A surviving photo in a scrapbook in the Library of Congress Houdini Collection suggests that this film had something to do with escaping from prison. Some years later, again for Pathé, he began a more determined assault with a fifteen-part serial, *The Master Mystery* —entitled in France *Le Maître du mystère*. It was shown internationally in the 1910s.[54]

One of the main characters in *The Master Mystery* was a robot —perhaps an unconscious echo of Robert-Houdin, who had made

From a Houdini scrapbook—1901 film activity (*Library of Congress*)

Poster for *Le Maître du mystère*, 15-part Pathé serial, 1910s (*Library of Congress*)

"automata" important characters in his magic theatre. The robot in *The Master Mystery* may have been the first such character in film, a forerunner of Hollywood's infatuation with them a half-century or so later.

The serial was a warm-up for Houdini. Beginning in 1919, he made in rapid succession five feature films: *The Grim Game* (1919), *Terror Island* (1920), *The Soul of Bronze* (1921), *The Man from Beyond* (1922), *Haldane of the Secret Service* (1923). He promoted them zealously with personal appearances. In the last two he invested his own funds, forming the Houdini Motion Picture Corporation for the purpose, and ended up losing some half-million dollars. The failure added a bitter note to his final years.[55]

In all his films the extraordinary feats for which he was celebrated became climaxes in fictional melodrama. In *The Master Mystery* he was hung upside down over a cauldron of bubbling acid, but freed himself. In *Terror Island* he rescued the heroine from a locked safe at the bottom of the sea; and while hanging from his neck, he freed himself from a torture rack devised by bloodthirsty natives. In *Haldane of the Secret Service,* gangsters threw him, tied and manacled, into a river, but he escaped and brought them to justice. In *The Man from Beyond* he was discovered frozen solid in a cake of ice in the Arctic, where he had apparently been for a hundred years; thawed, he resumed his life. Here his escapology slipped into the paranormal.

The plots were like those of countless films of the time. The difficulty was that Houdini was performing miracles such as many actors and actresses seemed able to perform in film after film. A subtitle in *Terror Island* assured audiences that Houdini "actually performed the amazing feats here pictured." It was a futile assurance, that could not unlock him from his fatal predicament. In film Houdini, like other magicians before him, was reducing his unique specialty almost to meaninglessness. Decades later, in the film *Houdini* (1953), Tony Curtis could do the magic.

Houdini poster, 1922   (*Library of Congress*)

HOUDINI PICTURE CORPORATION

presents

HOUDINI

in

"THE MAN FROM BEYOND"

HOUDINI

in
"The MAN FROM BEYOND"

Here's the weirdest, most uncanny, yet the most fascinating picture ever screened.

It tells a haunting romance—the story of a man who, after being frozen in a mass of Arctic ice for 100 years, is chopped out and returned to civilization to meet his reincarnated love of a century before.

And thrills! They crowd one upon the other reaching their climax in the rescue of the girl by Houdini on the very brink of Niagara Falls.

Positively the most daring rescue scene ever screened.

Note:—This picture comes direct from its sensational run at the Times Square Theatre, New York, at $2.00 prices.

Produced by Houdini Picture Corp.
(MENTION OTHER ATTRACTIONS HERE)
THEATRE NAME HERE
Two Column Ad Cut No. 103

Promotion items for *The Man from Beyond* (*Library of Congress*)

Houdini died in 1926. Toward the end he talked of starting a magic theatre in the United States, modeled after Egyptian Hall and the Robert-Houdin—but that tradition seemed to be expiring before the advance of movie palaces. The Robert-Houdin, a cinema in its last years, was torn down in 1923 to make way for the Boulevard Haussman. St. George's Hall, the final setting of England's Home of Mystery, had also become a cinema, and a few years later—in an appropriately symbolic takeover—became part of the British Broadcasting Corporation. Electronic magic was taking over.

We have sketched the careers of some of the magicians who plunged into cinema in its early years, with diverse results. There were others. In Leyda's *Dianying* we learn that the first film showing in Shanghai, China—August 11, 1896—was in conjunction with a magic act, but the act has not been identified.[56] The "father of Indian cinema," Dadasaheb Phalke, had been a magic performer; his genius for special effects may have owed something to this background.[57] In France the magician Claude Grivolas became a key figure in building the Pathé empire; Gaston Velle, conjurer and son of a conjurer, became Pathé's director of trick films.[58] In England, Jasper Maskelyne, grandson of the co-founder of Egyptian Hall, started out in the family tradition, became a skilled conjurer and illusionist, acquired a Vanishing Lady, and—in magic tradition—married her. But he had such an engaging stage presence that the motion pictures came after him, and he became a movie star instead.[59]

These magicians, known and unknown, constituted one of the many migrations that flowed into the cinema in its early years. There were also migrants from the world of invention, and from the theatre, the penny arcades, the fairgrounds, the lecture circuit. Among them the magicians were a fairly distinct group, but the groups all influenced each other, and the identity of each group was gradually lost. All had their impact on the evolution of a new industry.

The magicians were most active in the earliest years. What mark did they leave? What was their contribution? What sort of films did they make?

Nitrate Magic

I pursued a maiden and clasped a reed.
Gods and men, we are all deluded thus!

—Shelley

The record of the magic invasion can be traced through several stages. Fortunately a number of its films survive, even though theatrical films until midcentury were made on nitrate stock, unstable and combustible, and most early films have long since disintegrated, gone up in flames, or been destroyed. The fact that some survive is due to determined efforts of film archivists in many countries to salvage our world film heritage.

These efforts have included duplication of old nitrate films onto safety film—a slow and expensive process that will occupy many more years. Meanwhile many early films have also been *reborn*.

Until 1912 there was no legal provision in the United States for copyrighting a motion picture, but it was possible to copyright a *photograph*. In 1894 the Edison Company began the practice of making, on long strips of photographic paper, prints of Kinetoscope films and submitting the rolled-up strips as "photographs." Copyright law did not specify any official shape or proper dimensions for a "photograph," so the applications were accepted and a precedent established. During the next two decades about five thousand such rolls—"paper prints," they came to be called— arrived at the Library of Congress as copyright deposits. Some represented complete films; others included only representative shots or sequences. None could be projected or played on any available equipment. The "paper prints" were shelved and largely forgotten.

In the 1950s they began to stir new interest. Most of the films from which they had been made had long since perished. Meanwhile early films, as an aspect of our social history, commanded growing interest. Could new negatives possibly be made from the dried, often twisted rolls of paper? In Hollywood, Kemp R. Niver, film technician and collector of film memorabilia, began experiments to deal with the technical problems, which could only be solved by frame-by-frame copying. The time-consuming experiments were supported by the Academy of Motion Picture Arts and Sciences, and when the feasibility of the project was established, Congress appropriated funds to complete it.

As a result the Library of Congress acquired in the mid-1960s some three thousand pioneer films that had not existed for decades. The first years of film history thus had a strange rebirth. The reborn films, the Paper Print Collection, threw new light on many topics, including that of the magician in cinema. Scores of the films were found to relate to the work of magicians and the "trick film" genre they had set in motion. At least thirty Méliès films, some of which no longer existed in France and had been thought lost, turned up among the reborn films. So did a number of British-made trick films.[60]

In addition to what we know from the Paper Print Collection and from films duplicated directly from nitrate, we know the films of the period in other ways: through the promotional notes,

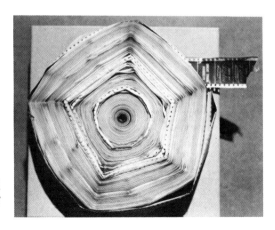

Paper print roll, dried and twisted (*Courtesy Kemp R. Niver*)

in some cases terse and in others marvelously overblown, in the catalogues of early companies; through comments in contemporary periodicals; and, as in the case of the Spanish-American naval battle of Smith and Blackton, through memoirs of film makers—which may be more showmanly than precise, but do give precious glimpses of irrecoverable days.

Thus a diversity of material, including a fair sampling of films, enables us to trace through various stages the role and impact of magicians in early film history.

New miracle. The first stage may have been the most successful. It was represented by the first film presentations of Trewey, Devant, Méliès, Hertz, and others, when the images themselves were the magic. Ironically, most of the short items were actuality bits—people leaving a factory, a crowd at Westminster Bridge, a baby being fed, a train entering a station. But the sequences were readily accepted as magic, as optical illusions—things appearing on a wall, that had no business being there. An astounding phenomenon, outdoing the magician's previous illusions—and perhaps the magician's supreme moment in his involvement with the motion picture.

Wizards on camera. In the next stage, magic entered the film itself in the person of the magician. Hindsight suggests this was a blunder, both for magic and for the art of film. But in the delirium of the hour it must have seemed essential that leading magicians, along with other performers—from parading royalty to serpentine dancers—should if possible be recorded by the camera and go out to the world, and perhaps to posterity, on film.

We have noted that David Devant, as early as June 1896, appeared in four films doing familiar stage specialties. Similar films were made by others, in various countries. In England, during 1896-98, they included John Nevil Maskelyne doing his plate-spinning; also Charles Bertram, known as England's "court conjurer," in his bravura patriotic act of pulling the flags of all nations out of an apparently empty hat and then transforming them into the Union Jack—a bit of chauvinistic magic echoed in the United States by an Edison Company film, *The Congress of Nations,* in which a magician "waves his hand and the flags of all nations slowly dissolve and blend into one huge American flag."[61] In 1898 Leopoldo Fregoli filmed his impersonations of Rossini and Verdi conducting orchestras—a film released in England by R. W. Paul.

By that time the idea of a filmed magic act was apparently losing lustre. A year later, when Fregoli appeared in the Méliès film entitled *The Lightning Change Artist*, involving his best-known specialty, he used camera trickery to make the stage marvels more marvelous. The same was true of Méliès in numerous on-camera performances as a magician. Thus the magician-on-camera genre was giving way to a newly evolving genre, the trick film, dedicated to exploiting the magic possibilities of film technology. For the moment, though, the figure of the performing magician remained in the picture.

This hybrid form—a filmed magic act beefed up by film trickery—is represented by some curious survivals in the Paper Print Collection: *The Magician* (1900), *Allabad the Arabian Wizard* (1902), *The Hindoo Fakir* (1902), *The Necromancer* (1903). The unidentified "magicians" in these films may or may not have been magicians. In all the films, it can be seen on close examination that the camera was stopped at crucial points to accomplish the transformations and other illusions. In other words, an on-camera magician no longer needed to be a magician. Magicians, by helping to create this form, had helped to make their own skills excess baggage.

As for the trick film, if it was to evolve, it needed above all to rid itself of the constricting setting of a performance—in other words, of the magician as the occasion for magic.

That his days in film were numbered is suggested by a 1904 promotional bulletin of the Biograph Company. Advertising a newly imported trick film, *The Bewitched Traveler*, the bulletin assured exhibitors there were no magicians in it.

The on-camera magic performance was probably the unhappiest venture of the magician in cinema. Few examples survive. Those made probably undermined the image the magician had for decades enjoyed.

It was in the trick film that magicians would make a contribution to film—not by appearing in film—though some still might—but by adapting to film their peculiar heritage of technical hanky-panky and finding new opportunities for it. They became important as film creators rather than as performers. The trick film vogue was short-lived, but sufficiently intense to spur wide imitation. Magicians and non-magicians participated in its moment of glory.

Inevitably many trick films echoed the grand moments of lead-

ing magicians. Some failed in the transplantation, others succeeded. But as we have seen, a doom haunted even the successes.
As any success was quickly imitated and mass-produced, success
tended to destroy itself by a rapid proliferation. So it was with
one of the most durable of nineteenth-century magic specialties
—the apparition.

Ghosts again. The spectacular, century-long successes of ghosts,
phantoms, skeletons, and other apparitions made it inevitable
that they should come to haunt the motion picture, and they
promptly did so. In 1898-99 the English technician G. A. Smith,
who later invented Kinemacolor—the first successful color process—unleashed a succession of short spirit films. Like most
films of the time, these were less than two minutes long. *The
British Film Catalogue 1895-1970* provides descriptions: [62]

> *The Corsican Brothers* (1898). Ghost of man's twin shows him
> vision of how he was killed in duel.

> *Faust and Mephistopheles* (1898). Satan conjures vision of
> girl, for whom old man signs pact and is made young.

> *Photographing a Ghost* (1898). Photographer tries to take pic-
> ture of a ghost, but it won't keep still and then vanishes.

> *The Gambler's Wife* (1899). Gambler is stopped from shooting
> himself by wife's spirit.

Walter Booth followed suit with similar films, as did others. In
Booth's *Undressing Extraordinary* (1899), a hotel guest finds a
skeleton in his bed; so does the traveler in the Edison film *Undressing Under Difficulties*, described in the company's 1902
catalogue. It is not surprising if the ghosts and skeletons soon
wore out their welcome. Their multiplication in early trick films
may finally have exorcised the public's long obsession with them.
At least for a time, the ghosts were laid to rest.

Vanishings. Sudden disappearances, like ghosts, had a hal-
lowed tradition in stage magic. Vanishings could involve any-
thing—watches, elephants, rabbits; but especially honored was
the Vanishing Lady. Robert-Houdin had had a Vanishing Lady,
made possible by a simple but extraordinarily effective trick cabinet. Other magicians imitated it; some contrived different methods and more spectacular effects. In the 1880s the magician
Buatier de Kolta introduced a new Vanishing Lady that is said to

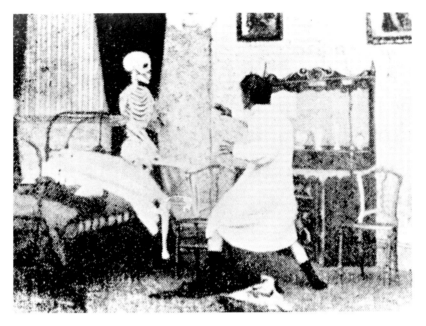

Undressing Extraordinary, ca. 1899—a Walter Booth trick film for Robert W. Paul (*National Film Archive, London*)

have baffled the magic profession as well as the public. A self-respecting illusionist was now expected to have a Vanishing Lady. All this made it certain that she would make an early appearance—and disappearance—in film.

Georges Méliès in his very first year of film making—1896—produced a film entitled *Vanishing Lady* and modeled after De Kolta. Perhaps sensing that a disappearance on film might not have the impact it had on stage, Méliès added a detail. The lady did not merely vanish, she turned into a skeleton.[63]

Startling as disappearances had always been, they were clearly too easy on film. Yet they had their film successes, based less on surprise than on narrative context. The hero of Hepworth's *The Bewitched Traveler* (1904) was bedeviled by a whole series of nightmarish disappearances that followed in helter-skelter sequence. As he breakfasts at an inn, his table fades away. Leaving the inn in consternation, he boards an omnibus, and the horses fade away. As he investigates this phenomenon, the bus and pas-

Robert-Houdin's Vanishing Lady

Illusion. We see a cabinet. Its bottom is off the floor; we can see underneath it. The cabinet is opened. The magician invites a few members of the audience to inspect its wood-paneled interior. They are then invited to seat themselves at the sides, to keep an eye on the area behind the cabinet. The Lady enters the cabinet, closing it. After an interval of banter, the magician opens the cabinet: the Lady has vanished. The doors are closed again. When they are reopened, the Lady has reappeared.

Explanation. After entering the cabinet, the Lady pulls toward her the hinged panels G, swinging them into the positions marked G1. The post P, which seemed to be a backstop for the cabinet doors, really serves to mask the meeting point of the swinging panels. The Lady is now at A, behind the panels. The sides of these panels facing outward (at a 45° angle) are mirrors. When the cabinet is reopened, the audience sees a reflection of the wood-paneled sides, but thinks it sees the back of the cabinet. The cabinet looks precisely as it did when empty.

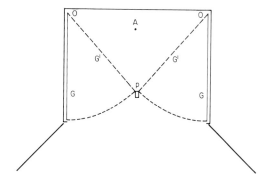

sengers fade away. He tries to take a train but it vanishes. Finally the traveler and his valise go up in a puff of smoke. The Biograph Company acquired American sales rights to this British film and copyrighted it, with the result that it survives in the Paper Print Collection.

Metamorphoses. Like the disappearance, the transformation had a history of magic success that made its film use inevitable. Biograph's early promotion bulletins list numerous short transformation items, each less than two minutes, from various sources: [64]

> *The Startled Lover* (1898). Girl turns to skeleton in lover's arms, but reappears again.
>
> *The Cremation* (1898). Girl is apparently burned to a skeleton, but comes back to life.
>
> *The X-Ray Mirror* (1899). Girl goes to mirror to try on hat; sees ballet girl, faints.
>
> *The Barber's Queer Customer* (1900). Man sits in barber's chair, and his face changes several times.
>
> *Pierrot and His Wives* (1900). How to make one fat wife out of two lean ones.
>
> *Five Minutes to Train Time* (1901). Baby is packed in a trunk, and comes out completely flattened.
>
> *The Price of a Kiss* (1902). Lady barber; customer tries to kiss her; sign on wall changes to read: "Kisses $1 extra."

Except for *The Cremation* and *The X-Ray Mirror*, all were copyrighted as paper prints and survive.

But transformations, like disappearances, needed firmer dramatic context to hold interest. A stage illusion created by David Devant in 1893, soon after his first appearance at Egyptian Hall, offered a formula echoed in innumerable early films. Entitled *The Artist's Dream*, his illusion involved a portrait on an easel that, in full view of the audience, turned into a living woman. Trick films were soon bringing all kinds of portraits to life. A surviving item of 1899:

> *The Poster Girls.* Chappie stands in front of bill-board; poster girls kick his hat off.[65]

Méliès used the device in many films, in rich and diverse ways. In *A Mysterious Portrait* (1899) Méliès is observing and appraising a photograph of himself, noting the baldness; the portrait then proceeds to observe and appraise him. In *A Spiritualist Photographer* a girl standing before a canvas turns into a painted image of herself, which the photographer—Méliès—then takes down and rolls up. When he later unrolls it, the painted image turns back into a girl. In *The Living Playing Cards* (1905) he plays similar games with playing cards, adding various other transformations. In the work of Méliès transformations often come in disorienting profusion, sometimes suggesting meanings but never dwelling on them.[66]

At Biograph the stream of trick films included a 1903 transformation item by its trick film specialist, Billy Bitzer. His *Welsh Rabbit* showed a girl at a chafing dish, carefully preparing a Welsh rarebit. After it cooks briefly, she lifts the cover for a peek and finds a live and kicking rabbit, which she takes out and fondles with great glee. Biograph's promotion bulletin stressed that

The Living Playing Cards, 1905—by Méliès   (*Museum of Modern Art, New York*)

she is "decollete" and "shown very large." Apparently it was feared that film trickery alone might not carry the day; or perhaps it was a carry-over from Mutoscope peepshow experience.[67]

Mayhem. It was in the magic tradition of decapitation, dismemberment, and other cheerful mayhem that the trick film found its firmest footing and substantial success. The satisfactions derived from such ghoulish games invite endless psychological probing. One pleasure seems to lie in the repudiation of all physical restrictions of human existence. In the world offered by the magician or the trick film, a severed head on a tray could engage in witty banter, severed limbs could reassemble and spring to life. It was macabre but cheerful, a combination that was part of the magic tradition, well exemplified by the act known as *The Decapitated Princess.* It made humans wildly resilient. The wide scope offered by film technology inspired new ways of exploiting this tradition. It eventually became a central ingredient in the appeal of the animated film.

Cheerful mayhem made an early debut in film. In a film surviving via the Paper Print Collection, *The Maniac Barber* (1899), a barber apparently finds his customer too restless, so he cuts the man's head off and finishes his work at a side counter. He then replaces the man's head. The customer indicates his complete satisfaction with the haircut, pays, and departs.[68] In *Up to Date Surgery* (1902) Méliès has similar frolic with a surgeon. The film does not seem to survive, but Paul Hammond in *Marvellous Méliès* summarizes the plot. A surgeon, having diagnosed a digestive malady, cuts his patient into small bits, then reassembles them wrongly, with ungainly results. But he muddles through, after which the patient, fully recovered, departs in high spirits.

In a number of films the joys of mayhem were associated with automobiles. Cecil Hepworth used his own first automobile for a trick film entitled *The Delights of Automobiling* (1903), which he felt confirmed popular feelings about the automobile. Discussing this years later, he explained: "The car was shown rushing along the road at its maximum speed of twelve miles an hour, when it suddenly explodes and blows its occupants sky high. A policeman immediately appears to investigate, and is just in time to find himself pelted with a shower of arms and legs and tires and wheels and things from the heavens. It was a very popular film and its profits nearly paid for the car."[69] Hepworth may also have used the car in *How To Stop a Car* (1902), in which a con-

ILLUSION OF THE DECAPITATED PRINCESS.

THE DECAPITATED PRINCESS—EXPLANATION OF ILLUSION.

The Decapitated Princess

Like the Vanishing Lady, the Decapitated Princess (and its numerous variants) used 45° angled mirrors. Under the Princess's head the audience thinks it sees to the back of the throne, but it actually sees a reflection of the similarly textured seat. The Princess rests her bosom on the back of the angled mirror; the rest of her is behind the throne. She takes this trick position at the moment the magician brings the "severed head" to the throne. His action masks the emergence of the real head. He must conceal the false head, which may for this purpose be a collapsible prop. In film all this ritual became obsolete. (*Library of Congress*)

95

stable on a country road tries to stop a speeding car by standing in the middle of the road. He is hit full and blown to fragments, but the fragments find each other and reassemble. A burly supervisor then shows the restored constable how it should be done. As the next speeding car approaches, the supervisor turns his back on it. Striking him full, it rebounds off the road and the culprits are arrested. The film survives in the National Film Archive of Britain.

In the transplantation to film, the world of severed heads and limbs was acquiring new ramifications. The determination of severed human parts to find each other and reunite was one such aspect. Another was an extravagant notion evolved by Devant and Méliès—apparently simultaneously—in films of 1898. Devant's film, made for a provincial tour and discussed in an interview in January 1899, showed a man who "cuts off his head and puts it down beside him. Another head, exactly like the first, appears on his shoulders. He cuts that off too, and he serves a third and a fourth the same way."[70] The multiple cloning obviously had bizarre possibilities, which Méliès was envisaging with similar relish and proceeded to exploit in a whole series of identical-heads films. In *The Four Troublesome Heads* (1898) a conjurer punishes three uncooperative heads that sing out of tune; he hits them with a banjo. In *Tit for Tat* (1904) one head badgers another. In *The King of the Sharpshooters* (1905) a rifleman uses five duplicates of his own head for target practice.[71]

Adding a further detail to the strange world, Méliès in *The Man with the Rubber Head* (1902) showed an experimenter— played by Méliès—who attaches a hose to a copy of his own head and inflates it. We see the head gasp and sputter as it swells. The experimenter, having tested the procedure to his satisfaction, lets an assistant take over, but the assistant pumps too vigorously, and the hugely inflated head explodes, smashing half the laboratory. Like many of Méliès's films, this film offered exceptional technical challenges. To portray the inflating of the head, Méliès's own head was photographed. He was seated in a chair which was dollied toward the camera—which was focused on the head with the lower part of the body masked. This series of images had to be superimposed, with the necessary masking, on footage of the pumping procedure.[72]

One of the most exuberant and endearing of decapitation films

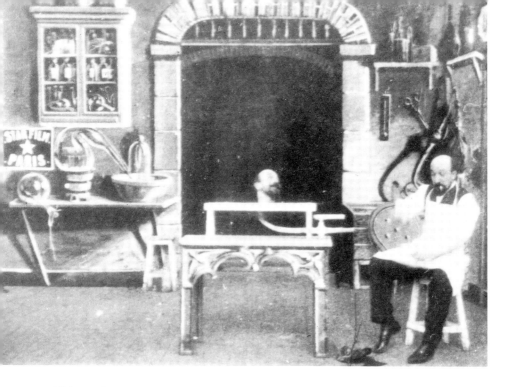

Méliès's *The Man with the Rubber Head,* 1902   (*Museum of Modern Art, New York*)

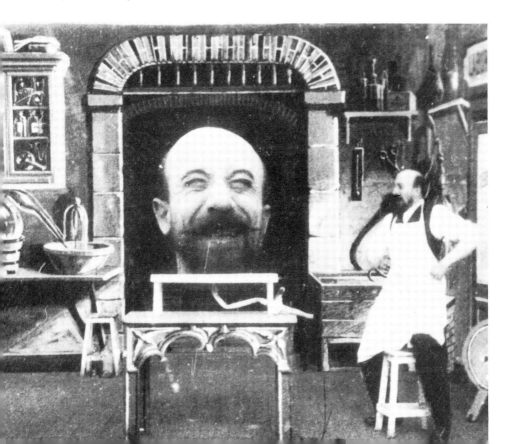

was *The Terrible Turkish Executioner* (1904), again by Méliès. Four doomed prisoners are brought before a public executioner. A plank with four holes, a sort of stock, is placed over their heads. The executioner, after flamboyant preparatory gestures, lops off all four heads with one mighty swoop of his huge scimitar. The headless bodies sit down together. The executioner dumps the severed heads into a barrel and goes back to his lunch. But one severed head floats up from the barrel and finds its body. Springing to life, the prisoner helps the other heads reunite with their respective parts. The executioner takes alarm and rises. But the prisoners have his great scimitar and with one swing divide him at the waist. The following moments, in which the severed upper half of his torso, wriggling on the floor, tries to "put on" the lower part—like a child learning to put on his pants—form a classic sequence of the trick film. The effort succeeds; the executioner springs to life and pursues the prisoners. Chorus girls dance in for a finale. Everyone is happy, as in most Méliès films.

In such films, as in the better known *A Trip to the Moon* (1902) and *The Impossible Voyage* (1904), trick drama was beginning to evolve extraordinary technical virtuosity. The many composite images required complex superimposures, with precise masking to achieve perfect fit. Masking often had to change from frame to frame. Careful calculations were needed to ensure the correct proportions of the various images. It is not surprising that John Brosnan, in *Movie Magic: The Story of Special Effects in Cinema*, finds their genesis in the trick film and especially in the work of Méliès.[73]

New tricks. Most technical devices that became characteristic of motion picture special effects—dissolves, fades, substitutions, double exposures, superimposures, masking, models, rear projections, mirrored images—were familiar to the first film magicians from a century of scientific magic. A few additional devices came from film itself. One was the reversal, a joyous game discovered by the very first projectionists. It provided a final fillip for early demonstrations of the Cinématographe and its rivals: A wall was torn down, and rebuilt itself. A horse jumped over a fence, then leaped back in reverse. A swimmer dove in, then popped out again. At first a projectionist's game, it became the basis for many trick films, such as G. A. Smith's *The Sandwiches* (1899). In this a man eats sandwiches in a restaurant, then refuses to pay. So the film is reversed and the restaurant gets its sandwiches back, intact. Another such film, *Reversing a Shave* (1905) showed a clean-shaven man carefully working with a razor. As he works, a beard gradually emerges.

In the Billy Bitzer film *Princess in the Vase* (1908)—a survivor via the Paper Print Collection—reversal plays an exceptionally interesting role. In ancient Egypt a princess, caught in an illicit love affair, is killed and cremated. We see the smoke from her funeral pyre mysteriously descending into a vase, which is then sealed and placed in her tomb. Centuries later the vase is in the hands of an American archaeologist, and is broken. The smoke escapes and metamorphoses back into the princess—with comic complications foreshadowing the television series, *I Dream of Jeannie*. An interesting sidelight is that the princess's lover is played by D. W. Griffith, shortly before his emergence as a director.

Likewise beginning as a game for projectionists, and later the basis for trick films, were slow motion (via high-speed photography) and accelerated motion (via low-speed photography). Walter Booth's *On a Runaway Motor Car Through Piccadilly Circus* (1899) offered audiences a dizzying "phantom ride" through busy London traffic—achieved by a quite sedate ride with the camera shooting very slowly, only a few frames per second.

Both slow motion and accelerated motion could have informational value. Thus Nevil Maskelyne's high-speed photography of artillery shells in flight is said to have enabled Britain's War Office to study their action in slow motion; and films recording the growth of plants via stop-motion—the ultimate form of low-speed photography—made it possible to view a weeks-long process of nature in a matter of seconds. Thus the technique of the trick film became a basic reference resource of documentary cinema.

A related use of stop-motion by a Biograph cameraman produced the remarkable *Demolishing and Building the Star Theatre* (1901). The month-long demolition of a New York theatre was photographed from a building across the street by a camera set to shoot only a few frames per hour. We see the theatre disappear in less than two minutes. The shadow of the building in which the camera is located sweeps across the demolition scene in regular rhythm, so that one can count the days. Since the shadow varies from sharp to fuzzy, we can observe weather changes. As a final flourish, the film maker added a reversal sequence, allowing the building to rise again.[74]

Another innovation derived from the possibilities of film, not from stage magic, was introduced by Walter Booth in *Upside Down, Or the Human Flies* (1899). The action was shot in a room in which the floor was painted like a ceiling, the ceiling like a floor, and furnishings arranged accordingly. Booth shot the action upside down, giving a perfect "human flies" illusion.

New directions. The pioneer trick film moved in many directions. A film with interesting Freudian overtones was *A Pipe Dream* (1905), shot by Billy Bitzer. A Biograph bulletin described it as follows:

> A novel picture showing a young woman smoking a cigarette and dreamily blowing the smoke over the palm of her hand. As she watches the smoke the figure of a young man appears kneeling on her hand and addressing her in passionate terms. The image seems to amuse her greatly, and she tries to catch it. It vanishes as her hand goes to seize it.[75]

She again blows smoke over her hand, apparently to coax the image back. But it does not return.

Another film credited to Bitzer involved a striking stop-motion experiment—in effect, a form of three-dimensional animation. In *The Sculptor's Nightmare* (1908) a sculptor receives commissions to make busts of various presidential candidates. Celebrating, he gets drunk and lands in jail. Sleeping there, he dreams of large masses of clay on pedestals, which take shape and become Bryan, Fairbanks, Taft, Theodore Roosevelt. They seem to come alive, smile, smoke cigars—then subside back into lumps of clay.

Several trick films involved J. Stuart Blackton in combinations of animation and live-action trickery. In *The Enchanted Drawing* (1900), perhaps a product of the Smith-Blackton magic team but made for Edison, we see Blackton at an easel drawing a cartoon face of a man, then drawing a wine bottle and a glass. Blackton apparently hankers for a drink and reaches for the bottle and glass, which become real as he does so. He drinks; the cartoon frowns, so Blackton pours another drink, giving the cartoon face a sip and causing the face to smile happily. Similar games are played with hats and a cigar.

A Pipe Dream, 1905—a Billy Bitzer trick film for Biograph   (*David Reese*)

The trick film had an early involvement with advertising. Méliès made a cigarette film using trickery similar to that of Blackton's *The Enchanted Drawing*. A Méliès advertising film for Dewar's Whiskey again used a "living portrait" technique. We see a stately home where Dewar's Whiskey is served. Family portraits descend from their frames to sample the drink.[76]

Perhaps inspired by advertising was the Pathé trick film *A Wonderful Hair Restorer* (1902), in which a barber is serving a customer with a magic nostrum guaranteed to grow hair. The treatment works. Not only does the customer get a bounteous crop of hair, but the barber gets long, bushy hairs growing from his hands.

The Enchanted Drawing, 1900.
Blackton gives his cartoon a drink—six frames from the paper print. The sequence represents less than a half-second of action. (*David Reese*)

Cigarette commercial—by Georges Méliès (*National Film Archive, London*)

For approximately a decade, devices of the trick film encouraged explorations of the fantastic, grotesque, impossible, and absurd—just as their special-effects descendants later focused on fantasies of the future, nightmares of the past, catastrophes of the present, and the magic potions and products of industry. But the appetite for film trickery seemed to be in decline by 1905. Films were becoming longer, more serious, more romantic. Handsome heroines and heroes were becoming central concerns. Motion pictures were turning into big business. It was an arena for giant corporations, not individual artisans.

The fortunes of Méliès, whose extraordinary output had included major delights of that first decade, declined at the same time. He made no films after 1913. The closing of theatres at the start of World War I helped bring him to ruin. The Théâtre Robert-Houdin later reopened, but not for long. Méliès gave his final performance there in 1920; three years later it was demol-

Georges Méliès in his kiosk, Gare Montparnasse, 1930　(*Museum of Modern Art, New York*)

ished. Ironically, the injection of film in 1896 had saved the magic theater and brought it a new prosperity, but in the long run contributed to its demise. By the mid-1920s magic theatres were a thing of the past. Late in life Georges Méliès and the second Mme. Méliès sold toys and candy in a kiosk in the Gare Montparnasse.

His career seemed to symbolize the brief hour of glory won by magicians in the world of film, and their final defeat. But the events can be seen in other ways also.

The appetites that drew crowds to magic theatres continued to be served—by movie palaces, Disneylands, radio, television, cable, satellites. Magic turned into "media." The artisans became an industry. The sense of continuity has perhaps been stronger than the sense of disruption.

The elements of magic are all there—the flights into the future, nightmares of the past, hopes that maintain us, fears that threaten, and all the mythologies that tell us of our heritage and destiny.

Does not our magic industry—via drama, documentary, docu-drama—still summon up ghosts of yesterday and use them for present purposes, whether of statecraft, religion, commerce? And is the industry not expected to show prudence as to what ghosts it summons, and to what effect? Are not our electron apparitions as ephemeral as images projected on smoke—and as changeable too, suiting their mien to time and place? Our magic industry is following where magicians led.

But as we look back on the magician's first encounter with cin-ema and those who flocked to see it, one question still haunts us: *How could those first audiences have thought of it as magic?*

Query

I thought this an artifice not to be despised: for we may in any chamber, if a man look in, see those things which were never there.

—della Porta, *Natural Magick,* 1558[77]

Perhaps the question must be turned around. How is it possible that we, who should know better, no longer think of the images of the magic industry as optical illusions, but have come to accept them as reality—our window on the world and what it thinks and does? Is this not astounding—perhaps alarming?

The magician is a figure of power. Throughout history he has played an ambiguous role, courted and also feared for his knowledge and apparent manipulation of mysterious forces. Often he was persecuted for sorcery and other abominations. Since the Renaissance he has gradually won a kind of freedom from intervention by allying himself with science, which was also winning an increasingly secure footing. The wonders he could perform, said the magician, came from the study of nature. He was a servant of nature. His magic was not black magic but "natural magic." It was not a manipulation but a demonstration and elucidation of natural wonders. Our oldest extant book on magic, *The Discoverie of Witchcraft,* by Reginald Scot, published in 1584, was written to assure readers that "natural magic" was good and worthy, a contribution to the appreciation and understanding of nature, and not to be confused—as the title page explains—with witchcraft and other "lewde," "impudent," and "pestilent" practices.

Throughout the nineteenth century the performer-magicians

The discouerie
of witchcraft,

Wherein the lewde dealing of witches
and witchmongers is notablie detected, the
knauerie of coniurors, the impietie of inchan-
tors, the follie of soothsaiers, the impudent fals-
hood of cousenors, the infidelitie of atheists,
the pestilent practises of Pythonists, the
curiositie of figurecasters, the va-
nitie of dreamers, the begger-
lie art of Alcu-
mystrie,

The abhomination of idolatrie, the hor-
rible art of poisoning, the vertue and power of
naturall magike, and all the conueiances
of Legierdemaine and iugling are deciphered:
and many other things opened, which
haue long lien hidden, howbeit
verie necessarie to
be knowne.

Heerevnto is added a treatise vpon the
nature and substance of spirits and diuels,
&c : all latelie written
by Reginald Scot
Esquire.

1. Iohn. 4, 1.

Beleeue not euerie spirit, but trie the spirits, whether they are
of God ; for manie false prophets are gone
out into the world, &c.

1584

In defense of "natural magic"—1584. Title page of *The Discoverie of Witchcraft* (i.e., the truth about witchcraft revealed). (*Library of Congress*)

maintained this stance, reiterating that their miracles were not really miracles but entertainment achieved by science, serving a wholesome and instructive purpose. Unfortunately, the performer-magicians were always shadowed by other magic practitioners, who *did* claim occult powers—mediums, spiritualists, and others. They too called up spirits. They produced phenomena that sometimes resembled the "illusions" of the performers. Throughout the century performer-magicians inveighed against spiritualists and declared themselves able to duplicate by scientific means any occult phenomena offered by spiritualists. The spiritualists assailed the performers as men of little faith—and slanderers. The struggle between them continued throughout the nineteenth century and into the twentieth. It involved leading magicians from Robert-Houdin to Houdini.

Unfortunately, the dividing line between the antagonists was never clear. The entertainer-magician said his miracles were products of science, but if devotees preferred to believe something more, the magician did not mind. His disclaimers sometimes took ambiguous forms, and he enjoyed his power over men's minds. And occasionally, if officialdom could be served and won thereby, he was willing to wrap his science in a mantle of the occult, as did Robert-Houdin with his bamboozling of the marabouts. Was he performing in Algeria as entertainer—or serving an official priestly function, keeping the ignorant in line?

Curiously, the periodical *Mahatma*, launched in 1895, proclaimed on its masthead that it was "the only paper in the United States devoted to the interests of magicians, spiritualists, mesmerists, etc." And its issue of October 1895 showed David Devant "and his spirit wife"—a magician using for publicity purposes a favorite device of spiritualists. Similarly, the British magazine *The Magician* described itself as "devoted to magic, spiritualism, hypnotism, and human progress." The rival groups were apparently so close in their interests that they could be served by the same trade press.

Today the magic performer has metamophosed into an industry which proclaims—as he did—that its purpose is entertainment, wholesome and instructive in effect. It says it is not exercising power, not trying to manipulate.

Yet what is this entertainment? Has it not become clear that the myths it projects, the news it selects, the products it promotes, tend to structure public attitudes on a whole host of issues? This

Mahatma.

THE ONLY PAPER IN THE UNITED STATES DEVOTED TO THE INTERESTS OF MAGICIANS, SPIRITUALISTS, MESMERISTS, ETC.

VOL. I. No. VIII.   NEW YORK, OCTOBER, 1895. · SINGLE COPY, 10 CENTS.

DAVID DEVANT AND HIS SPIRIT WIFE.

Mr. David Devant, now performing at Maskelyne & Cooke's Egyptian Hall, London, is so well known by reputation to all magicians the world over, that little can be said of this permanent engagement in the home of magic—Egyptian Hall. Among some of the most noted experiments that have originated from his fertile brain will be found the "Birth of Flora," "Vice-Versa," "Artist's Dream," etc. A bright future surely awaits this gentleman who has gained a footing in

clever magician that we do not already know. Mr. Devant is an originator as well as performer, and to this is due the reputation that he has gained, and which has given him a London that has never been accomplished by so young a man before, and he seems to be eminently qualified to attain still higher honors in the magical world. Mr. Devant is es-

Mahatma—for "magicians, spiritualists, mesmerists, etc. (*Library of Congress*)

A MONTHLY JOURNAL
DEVOTED TO MAGIC, SPIRITUALISM, HYPNOTISM, AND HUMAN PROGRESS.

No. 3.
Vol. 3.

February, 1907.
Entered at Stationer's Hall.

Price Fourpence.
By Post. 4½d.

PHAROS.

The *Magician*—devoted to "magic, spiritualism, hypnotism, and human progress." (*Library of Congress*)

power of "media" has generated a growing literature of concern. Meanwhile it has also generated more power.

It may well be that a central element in the power is the astonishing fact that media images are no longer seen by the public as optical illusions offered by magicians, but as something real. The unawareness is equivalent to defenselessness. The new industrialized magic may be closer to "black magic" than to "natural magic."

Perhaps we should heed Ingmar Bergman.[78] Born in a vicarage, he said he had an early familiarity with life and death behind the scenes. His father performed funerals, marriages, baptisms, and prepared sermons. The devil was an early acquaintance and created in the child's mind a need to personify him.

> This is where my magic lantern came in. It consisted of a small metal box with a carbide lamp—I can still remember the smell of the hot metal—and colored glass slides: Red Riding Hood and the Wolf, and all the others. And the Wolf was the Devil, without horns but a tail and a gaping red mouth, strangely real yet incomprehensible, a picture of wickedness and temptation on the flowered wall of the nursery.

At ten he acquired his first "rattling" film projector, and a film nine feet long, brown-colored, of a girl asleep in a meadow, who woke and stretched out her arms, and went off to the right. That was all. It was shown every night for years, until it broke and could no longer be mended.

> This little rickety machine was my first conjuring set. And even today I remind myself with childish excitement that I am really a conjurer, since cinematography is based on deception of the human eye. . . .

> When I show a film I am guilty of deceit. I use an apparatus which is constructed to take advantage of certain human weaknesses, an apparatus with which I can sway my audience in a highly emotional manner—make them laugh, scream with fright, smile, believe in fairy stories, become indignant, feel shocked, charmed, deeply moved or perhaps yawn with boredom. Thus I am an impostor or, when the audience is willing to be taken in, a conjurer. I perform conjuring tricks with apparatus so expensive and so wonderful that any entertainer in history would have given anything to have it.

Notes

1. Robert-Houdin, *Memoirs of Robert-Houdin*, pp. 266-68.
2. Maskelyne, *White Magic*, p. 90.
3. Barnes, *Optical Projection*, pp. 10-11.
4. For techniques and influence of *Fantasmagorie* see Robertson, *Mémoires récréatifs; Magasin Pittoresque*, XXVII, pp. 51-52, 1859; Barnes, *Optical Projection*, pp. 27-28; Goldston, *A Magician's Swan Song*, pp. 20-22.
5. Pecor, *The Magician on the American Stage*, pp. 106, 170.
6. Odell, *Annals of the New York Stage*, III, pp. 165, 697. Apparently Robertson was by this time better known for his other experimental ventures. Odell refers to him as "the balloonist."
7. Burlingame, *History of Magic and Magicians*, p. 7; Christopher, *Panorama of Magic*, pp. 41-42, 137. Oehler, *Life, Adventures, and Unparalleled Sufferings*, pp. 222-23. Oehler was in Paris during Robertson's great successes there. Like Robertson, Oehler took up ballooning, doing frequent balloon-flight demonstrations.
8. Odell, *Annals of the New York Stage*, II, p. 302.
9. Brewster, *Letters on Natural Magic*, pp. 64-69, 81. The twentieth-century magician and magic historian Will Goldston, writing on the persistent popularity of the technology, wrote: "For a considerable time, we find that the age-old idea of projecting images on to a smoke screen was the only real illusion in use. It was an illusion that was admirably suited to the convenience of the conjurer. To make the images disappear it was only necessary to damp down the smoke. . . . It was an illusion that was easily worked, yet not easily detected." Goldston, *A Magician's Swan Song*, p. 22.
10. Dircks, *The Ghost!*, pp. 77-78.
11. Houdini traced the beginnings of "spirit photography" to 1862, in the work of a Boston spiritualist. Houdini, *A Magician Among the Spirits*, p. 117.
12. Barnes, *Optical Projection*, p. 31.
13. *The Magic Lantern*, V, p. 5, May 1879.

14. Hepworth, *Came the Dawn,* pp. 15-18.
15. For a detailed account of the invention and brief career of the Kinetoscope see Hendricks, *The Kinetoscope.*
16. Barnes, *The Beginnings of Cinema in England,* p. 29.
17. Several excellent sources on Méliès are available, especially: Hammond, *Marvellous Méliès,* which provides a complete filmography on the work of Méliès; and Frazer, *Artificially Arranged Scenes,* which lists extant films and the major archives where they are available. This section is based largely on these studies; other sources as noted. For an illuminating panorama of the period and influences on Méliès, see Deslandes, *Le Boulevard du cinéma à l'époque de Georges Méliès.*
18. Méliès, "Mes Mémoires," in Bessy and Duca, *Georges Méliès, Mage* (appendix); Sadoul, *Georges Méliès,* p. 14.
19. Malthête-Méliès, *Méliès l'enchanteur,* pp. 140-41.
20. This section is based largely on Andrieu (ed.), *Souvenirs des Frères Isola;* other sources as noted.
21. Derval, *The Folies Bergère,* pp. 45-46.
22. Messter, *Mein Weg mit dem Film,* p. 10. The date was April 26, 1896, a few days before the first Lumière showing in Berlin. According to Messter, the Isola system for advancing the film proved unsatisfactory.
23. Barnes, *Precursors of the Cinema,* p. 16.
24. *Ibid.,* p. 19.
25. Devant, *My Magic Life,* pp. 70-71.
26. Maskelyne, *White Magic,* pp. 127-29.
27. Paul, *Before 1910,* p. 4.
28. Hertz, *A Modern Mystery Merchant,* pp. 23-25.
29. *Ibid.,* p. 29.
30. *Ibid.,* p. 180.
31. *Ibid.,* p. 140.
32. Baxter, *The Australian Cinema,* pp. 1-3.
33. *Times of India,* September 15, 1897; December 26, 1898.
34. *Era,* July 16, 1898.
35. Wasson, *The Beginning of Film in Australia,* p. 1.
36. Leyda, *Dianying,* p. 2.
37. Christopher, *The Illustrated History of Magic,* p. 129.
38. Nohain, *Frégoli,* p. 82.
39. *Ibid.,* p. 83; Hammond, *Marvellous Méliès,* p. 42. Some Fregoli film survives at the Cineteca Nazionale, Rome.
40. According to Victor, the purchase of the Cinématographe was in 1896, which seems at odds with Lumière annals. Victor's recollection of the date may be wrong, or the purchase may have involved one of many imitations. The date discrepancy is discussed by David Shepard in his valuable monograph *The Victor Anima-*

tograph Company, the main source for this biographical summary. Other sources as noted.

41. Ramsaye, *A Million and One Nights*, pp. 349-50. Ramsaye gives Victor's stage name as "The Great Victor."
42. Shepard, *The Victor Animatograph Company*, p. 25.
43. Perry, *The Great British Picture Show*, pp. 22-23.
44. Paul, *Before 1910*, pp. 5-6. For details on the Paul-Booth trick films see especially Talbot, *Moving Pictures*.
45. Bitzer, *Billy Bitzer: His Story*, p. 8.
46. *Ibid.*, p. 9. See Hendricks, *The Beginnings of the Biograph*, for the evolution of the company.
47. The section is based mainly on Anthony Slide's authoritative account of the history of the Vitagraph Company, *The Big V;* other sources as noted.
48. Ramsaye, *A Million and One Nights*, p. 275.
49. Blackton's comments are from a talk at the University of Southern California, quoted, Slide, *The Big V*, pp. 5-7.
50. *Mahatma*, February 1899.
51. Smith, *Two Reels and a Crank*, pp. 66-67.
52. Curiously, Slide's carefully researched *The Big V*, pp. 9-10, refers to this vanished film as *The Battle of Manila Bay;* whereas Smith in *Two Reels and a Crank*, p. 68, refers to it as *The Battle of Santiago Bay*. It could presumably have served as either, or both, and perhaps did. By both accounts, it was received with enthusiasm at New York vaudeville theatres.
53. Christopher, *Houdini: The Untold Story*, pp. 55-56.
54. The individual episodes had dramatic titles of their own: "The Madagascar Menace," "The Death Noose," "The Flash of Death," etc.
55. For Houdini's financial problems see Christopher, *Houdini: The Untold Story*, p. 262. Goldston, *Sensational Tales of Mystery Men*, p. 125, quotes comments by Houdini on the film losses.
56. Leyda, *Dianying*, p. 1.
57. Barnouw and Krishnaswamy, *Indian Film*, pp. 10, 16.
58. Deslandes and Richard, *Histoire comparée du cinéma*, II, pp. 299-303, 318-21.
59. See Maskelyne, *White Magic*, for both his magic and film reminiscences.
60. Niver, *Motion Pictures from the Library of Congress Paper Print Collection 1894-1912*, recounts the evolution of the project and synopsizes some 3000 films.
61. The Charles Bertram film is mentioned in Low and Manvell, *The History of the British Film*, I, p. 77; *The Congress of Nations* is described in the 1902 catalogue *Edison Films*, p. 95.
62. Gifford, *The British Film Catalogue 1895-1970*.

63. Hammond, *Marvellous Méliès*, p. 30.
64. From *Biograph Bulletins*. The dates here listed are production dates determined by Niver from technical and other evidence. Copyright dates were in many cases later. See chart, *Biograph Bulletins*, pp. 423-54.
65. *Ibid.*, p. 62.
66. Hammond, *Marvellous Méliès*, p. 90; Frazer, *Artificially Arranged Scenes*, pp. 26, 75, 151-54.
67. *Biograph Bulletins*, p. 88.
68. In England J. Williamson's *The Clown Barber* apparently followed an identical sequence and may have been first. See Low and Manvell, *The History of the British Film*, I, p. 79.
69. Hepworth, *Before 1910*, pp. 10-11.
70. *Today*, January 28, 1899. Included in Houdini Scrapbook No. 22, Library of Congress.
71. Hammond, *Marvellous Méliès*, pp. 100-101.
72. *Ibid.*, p. 100; Frazer, *Artificially Arranged Scenes*, pp. 91-93.
73. Brosnan, *Movie Magic*, pp. 15-19.
74. The reversal sequence, mentioned in Biograph promotion, is not included in the paper print copy deposited for copyright in 1902. See *Biograph Bulletins*, p. 70; and Niver, *Motion Pictures from the Library of Congress Paper Print Collection*, p. 158.
75. *Biograph Bulletins*, p. 21.
76. Hammond, *Marvellous Méliès*, pp. 35-36.
77. Porta, *Natural Magick*, p. 370.
78. The section is based on Bergman's introduction to *Four Screenplays*, pp. xiv-xv.

Bibliography

Books

Allen, John. *The Magic Lantern: Its Principles, and How To Use It.* New York, De Witt, undated.

Andrieu, Pierre (ed.). *Souvenirs des Frères Isola.* Paris, Flammarion, 1943.

Barnes, John. *The Beginnings of Cinema in England.* London, David and Charles, 1976.

Barnes, John. *Optical Projection.* Part II of *Catalogue* of Barnes Museum of Cinematography. St. Ives (England), Barnes Museum, 1970.

Barnes, John. *Precursors of the Cinema.* Part I of *Catalogue* of Barnes Museum of Cinematography. St. Ives (England), Barnes Museum, 1970.

Barnouw, Erik, and S. Krishnaswamy. *Indian Film,* 2nd Edition. New York, Oxford University Press, 1980.

Baxter, John. *The Australian Cinema.* Sydney, Pacific Books, 1970.

Beck, Leonard N. "Things Magical," in *Quarterly Journal of the Library of Congress,* October 1974.

Bellachini in der Westentasche; oder, Zauberer und Hexenmeister der Neuzeit. Berlin, Beuckert & Radetzki, undated.

Bergman, Ingmar. *Four Screenplays.* Translated from Swedish by Lars Malmstrom and David Kushner. New York, Simon and Schuster, 1960.

Bessy, Maurice. "Georges Méliès," in *Anthologie du Cinéma,* Vol. II. Paris, L'Avant-Scène, 1967.

Bessy, Maurice, and L. Duca. *Georges Méliès, mage* (including "Mes Mémoires," by Méliès). Paris, Prisma, 1945. Reprinted, Pauvert, 1961.

Biograph Bulletins 1896-1908. Compiled by Kemp R. Niver. Los Angeles, Locare Research Group, 1971.

Bitzer, G. W. *Billy Bitzer: His Story.* New York, Farrar, Straus and Giroux, 1973.

Brewster, Sir David. *Letters on Natural Magic: Addressed to Sir Walter Scott, Bart.* London, J. Murray, 1832: New York, Harper, 1842.

British Film Catalogue 1895-1970. See Gifford, Denis.

Brosnan, John. *Movie Magic: The Story of Special Effects in the Cinema.* Revised edition. New York, New American Library, 1976.

Burlingame, H. J. *History of Magic and Magicians.* Chicago, Charles L. Burlingame, 1895.

Ceram, C. W. *Archaeology of the Cinema.* New York, Harcourt Brace & World, undated.

Chanan, Michael. *The Dream That Kicks: The Prehistory and Early Years of Cinema in Britain.* London, Routledge & Kegan Paul, 1980.

Chavigny, Jean. *Robert-Houdin, Rénovateur de la magie blanche.* Undated.

Christopher, Milbourne. *Houdini: A Pictorial Life.* New York, Crowell, 1976.

Christopher, Milbourne. *Houdini: The Untold Story.* New York, Crowell, 1969.

Christopher, Milbourne. *The Illustrated History of Magic.* New York, Crowell, 1973.

Christopher, Milbourne. *Panorama of Magic.* New York, Dover, 1962.

Clarke, Sidney Wrangel. *The Annals of Conjuring.* London, George Johnson, 1929.

Colombon, Henri. *Trewey, Premier Shadowgraphiste, mime, et comédien.* Carpentras, Batailler, 1909.

Dawes, Edwin A. *The Great Illusionists.* London, David and Charles, 1979.

Derval, Paul. *The Folies Bergère.* Translated from French by Lucienne Hill. London, Methuen, 1955.

Deslandes, Jacques. *Le Boulevard du cinéma à l'époque de Georges Méliès.* Paris, Éditions du Cerf, 1963.

Deslandes, Jacques. *Histoire comparée du cinéma,* Vol. I. Casterman, 1966.

Deslandes, Jacques, and Jacques Richard. *Histoire comparée du cinéma,* Vol. II. Casterman, 1968.

Devant, David. *My Magic Life.* London, Hutchinson, 1931.

De Vaulabelle, A., and C. Hemardinquer. *La Science du théâtre.* Paris, Paulin, 1908.

Dircks, Henry. *The Ghost! As Produced in the Spectre Drama: Popu-*

larly Illustrating the Marvellous Optical Illusions Obtained by the Apparatus Called the Dircksian Phantasmagoria. London, Spon, 1864.

Dolbear, A. E. *The Art of Projecting.* Boston, Lee & Shepard, 1876.

Edison Films. Catalogue. West Orange, N.J., 1902.

Evans, Henry Ridgely. *Magic and Its Professors.* Philadelphia, McKay, 1902.

Evans, Henry Ridgely. *The Old and the New Magic.* Chicago, Open Court, 1906.

Fischer, Lucy. "The Lady Vanishes," in *Film Quarterly,* Fall 1979.

Foster, R. B. *Hopwood's Living Pictures.* (New edition of Hopwood, *Living Pictures,* 1899.) London, Hatton, 1915.

Frazer, John. *Artificially Arranged Scenes: The Films of Georges Méliès.* Boston, G. K. Hall, 1979.

Fregoli, Leopoldo. *Fregoli Racontato da Fregoli.* Milan, Rizzoli, 1936.

Gernsheim, Helmut, with Alison Gernsheim. *The History of Photography: From the Earliest Use of the Camera Obscura in the Eleventh Century to 1914.* New York, Oxford University Press, 1955.

Gifford, Denis. *The British Film Catalogue 1895-1970.* New York, McGraw-Hill, 1973.

Goldston, Will. *A Magician's Swan Song.* London, John Long, undated.

Goldston, Will. *Sand, Smoke and Rag Pictures.* London, The Magician, undated (*ca.* 1912).

Goldston, Will. *Secrets of Famous Illusionists.* London, John Long, 1933. Republished, Ann Arbor, Gryphon, 1971.

Goldston, Will. *Sensational Tales of Mystery Men.* London, Goldston, 1929.

Goldston, Will. *Will Goldston's Who's Who in Magic.* London, Goldston, 1934.

Hall, Trevor. *Old Conjuring Books: A Bibliographical and Historical Study with a Supplementary Checklist.* London, Duckworth, 1972.

Hammond, Paul. *Marvellous Méliès.* London, Gordon Fraser, 1974.

Hampton, Benjamin B. *History of the American Film Industry: From Its Beginnings to 1931.* New York, Covici Friede, 1931; Dover, 1970.

Hendricks, Gordon. *The Beginnings of the Biograph.* New York, The Beginnings of the American Film, 1964.

Hendricks, Gordon. *The Kinetoscope.* New York, The Beginnings of the American Film, 1966.

Hepworth, Cecil M. *Before 1910: Kinematograph Experiences.* Proceedings of the British Kinematograph Society, No. 38, 1936.

Hepworth, Cecil M. *Came the Dawn: Memories of a Film Pioneer.* London, Phoenix, 1951.

Hertz, Carl. *A Modern Mystery Merchant: The Trials, Tricks and Travels of Carl Hertz, the Famous American Illusionist.* London, Hutchinson, 1924.

Hopkins, Albert A. *Magic: Stage Illusions and Scientific Diversions, Including Trick Photography.* New York, Munn, 1898. Reprinted, Blom, 1967; Dover, 1976.

Hopwood, Henry. *Living Pictures: Their History, Photoduplication and Practical Working.* London, Optician and Photographic Trades Review, 1899. New edition as *Hopwood's Living Pictures*, by R. B. Foster. London, Hatton, 1915.

Houdini, Harry. *A Magician Among the Spirits.* New York, Harper, 1924.

Houdini, Harry. *The Unmasking of Robert-Houdin.* London, Routledge, 1909.

Jenness, George A. *Maskelyne and Cooke: Egyptian Hall, London, 1873-1904.* Enfield (Middlesex, England), 1967.

Kircher, Athanasius. *Ars Magna Lucis et Umbrae.* Rome, 1646.

Leyda, Jay. *Dianying: Electric Shadows. An Account of Films and the Film Audience in China.* Cambridge (Mass.), MIT Press, 1972.

Low, Rachael, and Roger Manvell. *The History of the British Film,* Vol. 1 (1896-1906). London, Allen & Unwin, 1949.

MacGowan, Kenneth. *Behind the Screen: The History and Techniques of the Motion Picture.* New York, Delta, 1965.

The Magic Lantern: How To Buy and How To Use It, and How To Raise a Ghost ("by A Mere Phantom"). London, Houlston, 1880.

Malthête-Méliès, Madeleine. *Méliès l'enchanteur.* Paris, Hachette, 1973.

Marion, Fulgence. *L'Optique.* 3rd Edition. Paris, Hachette, 1874. Translated into English by Charles W. Quin as *The Wonders of Optics.* New York, Scribner, 1869. Microfilm.

Maskelyne, Jasper. *Magic—Top Secret.* London, Stanley Paul, 1949.

Maskelyne, Jasper. *White Magic: The Story of the Maskelynes.* London, Stanley Paul, 1936.

McKechnie, Samuel. *Popular Entertainments Through the Ages.* London, Sampson Low, Marston & Co.; New York, Blom, 1969.

Méliès, Georges. "Mes Mémoires," in Maurice Bessy and Lo Duca, *Georges Méliès, mage.* Paris, Prisma, 1945. Reprinted, Pauvert, 1961.

Messter, Oskar. *Mein Weg mit dem Film.* Berlin, Hesse, 1936.

Narath, Albert. *Oskar Messter, der Begründer der deutsche Kino und Filmindustrie.* Berlin, Deutsche Kinemathek, 1966.

National Film Archive Catalogue, Part III: Silent Fiction Films 1895-1930. Foreword by J. B. Priestley. London, British Film Institute, 1966.

Niver, Kemp R. *The First Twenty Years: A Segment of Film History.* Los Angeles, Locare Research Group, 1968.

Niver, Kemp R. *Motion Pictures from the Library of Congress Paper Print Collection 1894-1912.* Berkeley and Los Angeles, University of California Press, 1967.

Niver, Kemp R. (compiler). *Biograph Bulletins.* See *Biograph Bulletins 1896-1908.*

Nohain, Jean. *Frégoli, 1867-1936: Sa Vie et ses sécrets.* Paris, Jeune Parque, 1968.

Odell, George C. D. *Annals of the New York Stage,* Vol. II (1798-1821). New York, Columbia University Press, 1927.

Odell, George C. D. *Annals of the New York Stage,* Vol. III (1821-1834). New York, Columbia University Press, 1928.

Oehler, Andrew. *The Life, Adventures, and Unparalleled Sufferings of Andrew Oehler.* Trenton (N.J.), Oehler, 1811.

Paul, Robert W. *Before 1910: Kinematograph Experiences.* Proceedings of the British Kinematograph Society, No. 38, 1936.

Pecor, Charles Joseph. *The Magician on the American Stage.* Ph.D. dissertation. Athens, University of Georgia, 1976. Microfilm.

Pepys, Samuel. *The Diary of Samuel Pepys,* ed. by Robert Latham and William Matthews. Vol. VII (1666). Berkeley, University of California Press, 1972.

Perry, George. *The Great British Picture Show: From the 90's to the 70's.* New York, Hill & Wang, 1974.

Porta, Giovanni Battista della. *Natural Magick.* English translation (of *Magiae Naturalis,* 1558) printed in London, 1658; facsimile edition, New York, Basic Books, 1957.

Quigley, Martin, Jr. *Magic Shadows: The Story of the Origin of the Motion Picture.* Washington, Georgetown University Press, 1948.

Ramsaye, Terry. *A Million and One Nights: A History of the Motion Picture.* New York, Simon and Schuster, 1926.

Reade, Eric. *Australia's Silent Films.* Melbourne, Lansdowne, 1970.

Robert-Houdin, Jean Eugène. *Memoirs of Robert-Houdin.* Translated from the French by Lascelles Wraxall, with a New Introduction and Notes by Milbourne Christopher. New York, Dover, 1964.

Robertson, Étienne Gaspard. *Mémoires récréatifs, scientifiques et anecdotiques.* Paris, 1831.

Rossi, Paolo. *Francis Bacon: From Magic to Science.* Translated by Sacha Rabinovitch. Chicago, University of Chicago Press, 1968.

Sadoul, Georges. *Georges Méliès.* Paris, Édition Seghers, 1961.

Sardina, Maurice. *Where Houdini Was Wrong.* Translation, by Victor Farelli, of *Les Erreurs de Harry Houdini.* London, George Armstrong, 1950.

Scot, Reginald. *The Discoverie of Witchcraft.* London, 1584. New York, Dover, 1972.

Shepard, David H. *The Victor Animatograph Company: And the Genesis of Non-Theatrical Film.* Davenport (Iowa), Shepard, 1975.

Slide, Anthony. *The Big V: A History of the Vitagraph Company.* Metuchen (N.J.), Scarecrow Press, 1976.

Smith, Albert E., in conjunction with Phil A. Koury, *Two Wheels and a Crank.* Garden City (N.Y.), Doubleday, 1952.

Talbot, F. A. *Moving Pictures: How They Are Made and Worked.* London, Heinemann, 1912, 1923.

Wasson, Mervyn. *The Beginning of Film in Australia.* Carlton, Australian Film Institute, 1965.

Webb, James (ed.). *The Mediums and the Conjurers.* New York, Arno, 1976.

Winter, Marian Hannah. *The Theatre of Marvels.* New York, Benjamin Blom, 1962.

Periodicals

Electronic Engineering. London, 1928-

Era, The. London, 1868-

Magasin Pittoresque, Le. Paris, 1833-

Magic. London, 1900-

Magic Lantern, The. Philadelphia, 1874-

Magician, The. Liverpool, 1904-

Magic Wand and Magical Review. London, 1910-

Mahatma. New York, 1895-

M.U.M. (Magic-Unity-Might). New York, 1911-

Phonoscope, The. New York, 1896-

Scientific American. New York, 1845-

Sphinx, The. Chicago, etc., 1902-

Wizard, The. London, 1905-

Index

123